NORTH DEVON CLAY

At Marland works in the early years of the twentieth century. PETER *has brought workmen back from the moors while* MARY *waits to take them on to Torrington at the end of the working day. The large extent of the works is apparent, from the engine and boiler house on the left to the covered drying floors on the right. One of the terra cotta kilns is prominent behind the circular roofed engine shed.*
E. A. HOLWILL

NORTH DEVON CLAY

The story of an industry and its railways

BY

MICHAEL MESSENGER

TWELVEHEADS PRESS

TRURO 2007

CONTENTS

Introduction		5
Chapter 1	- The Beginnings of an Industry	7
Chapter 2	- The Marland Works and the North Devon Clay Company	9
Chapter 3	- The Torrington & Marland Railway	25
Chapter 4	- John Barraclough Fell and the Viaducts	41
Chapter 5	- Locomotives and Rolling Stock of Marland	47
Chapter 6	- Standard Gauge Proposals	65
Chapter 7	- The North Devon & Cornwall Junction Light Railway	69
Chapter 8	- A Southern Branch Line	79
Chapter 9	- The Meeth Works	91
Chapter 10	- Locomotives and Rolling Stock of Meeth	99
Chapter 11	- The 21st Century	102
Appendix 1	- Contract and Specification of the Torrington & Marland Railway	103
Appendix 2	- Operating Costs of the Torrington & Marland Railway	108
Appendix 3	- Locomotives of Marland and Meeth	109
Appendix 4	- Anderson's Sale	110
Acknowledgements		112
Index		116

Front cover main picture: *The train from Torrington waits at Summit to be taken on to the works by* MARLAND, *probably soon after the Great War.* COLLECTION B. D. HUGHES

Front cover other pictures left to right: *E1R 2696 leaves Torrington, 1936.* R. W. KIDNER
The first underground level at Woolladon in 1927. ECC BALL CLAYS
10-ton wagon at Marland works. NORTH DEVON CLAY CO.

Back cover : *The back cover of an advertising booklet produced by the North Devon Clay Co. about 1900 provides an apt summary.* BALL CLAY HERITAGE SOCIETY

Units of measurement and money used in this book are those which were concurrent with events described. They may be converted as follows:
Money: £1 =   20 shillings (s) = 100 pence (p)
                       1 guinea = 21 shillings
                       1 shilling = 12 pence (d)
Length: 1 mile = 8 furlongs = 80 chains = 1,760 yards = 1.6093 kilometres
                       1 yard = 3 feet = 36 inches = 0.9144 metres
                       1 fathom = 6 feet
Weight: 1 ton = 20 hundredweight (cwt) = 1.016 tonnes

All rights reserved. No part of this publication may be reproduced or transmitted in any form or by any means without the prior permission of the publisher.
© Michael Messenger 2007.

TWELVEHEADS PRESS

First published 1982 and this edition 2007 by Twelveheads Press
Truro, Cornwall.
ISBN 978 0 906294 65 9
British Library Cataloguing-in-Publication Data.
A catalogue record for this book is available from the British Library.
Printed by The Amadeus Press Ltd., Cleckheaton, West Yorkshire.

INTRODUCTION

Lying between the granite heights of Dartmoor and the ocean swell of Bideford Bay is a corner of Devon that was once little known either to the tourist or to many Devonians. The principal industry is agriculture and the pastoral landscape is pleasant but undramatic, and until recently there were few attractions for those who did not have business here. But between Great Torrington and Hatherleigh, to narrow the field of view, by an instance of geological good fortune, nature has deposited a mineral of use and value to man. The mineral is ball clay and the exploitation of this substance, and in particular its transport, is the subject of this book.

To be frank this book was not intended. I was initially curious as to how a well known international engineer became involved in a minor Devon industrial railway and, as well as gaining an insight into the engineer himself, I was pleasantly surprised to find a narrow gauge railway full of character. It is worth noting here that the Torrington & Marland Railway, as a working narrow gauge railway, lasted 44 years, rather longer than that better known Devon narrow gauge railway, the Lynton & Barnstaple. The story of the clay industry was so closely linked that it was impossible to exclude it, not that one would have wished to. The North Devon & Cornwall Junction Light Railway deserved a mention as the replacement of the Torrington & Marland Railway but this too grew in stature as I learned of its lengthy, and often amusing, pre-history and of how a simple light railway became a matter of political importance. Its chapter could be subtitled 'a catalogue of disappointments'. The Meeth working had strong links with those at Marland and with the NDCJLR, and it would have been churlish and unworthy not to have told their story also.

And so the project grew. With so much information coming to hand the metamorphosis

AVONSIDE appears to be propelling this train across the Torridge Viaduct towards Marland. The lack of passengers suggests it is going to pick up the clay workers at the end of the day. The pier on the left bank still survives.
JOHN ALSOP
COLLECTION

to a book became inevitable. The transport aspect is my particular penchant but it soon became apparent that transport was a very important factor in the development of the industry. Whilst the Marland workings begat the narrow gauge railway in 1881 the workings could not have survived without it, and similarly the Meeth enterprise would soon have failed had not the NDCJLR been successfully built. (Whether the quarter-million pound NDCJLR can be described as successful from any other viewpoint is doubtful.) No apology is offered, therefore, for the emphasis on railway history in this industrial history for the one is part of the other and inseparable. That the transport story has proved so fascinating and full of interest is a bonus.

In the near quarter of a century since this book was first published much has changed. Looking back now, I realise how fortunate I have been to have seen both the clay companies operating by the 'old methods' and to have experienced first hand the various railways. Modern progress has altered the clay industry and closed the railways. But the leisure and tourism industries have grown; most of the route of the railways is now the Tarka Trail and sees more 'passengers' than it ever did as a railway.

Apart from happenings since the first edition not a great deal of significant additional source material has come to hand to add to the story. The National Archives have released more files and some quite useful titbits regarding the railways have been found, particularly in photographs which have revealed much that is otherwise unrecorded. We do know a lot more about the activities of J. B. Fell, thanks to the efforts of my good friend Ted Wade, sadly now deceased, but much relates to Fell's work in other railway spheres. It is not the place here to dwell on these or on nebulous 'might-have-beens'. I have taken the opportunity to add earlier research which was not included in the first edition.

A railway that is incorporated by Act of Parliament - such as the Torrington & Okehampton Railway - or by a Light Railway Order - the North Devon & Cornwall Junction Light Railway - has a formal and legal title but a railway built on private land by an individual for his own purposes does not necessarily, unless he chooses to give it one. The Torrington & Marland Railway was such a railway and was known by a variety of names, even by its owners; the Marland Railway, the Marland Light Railway, the North Devon Clay Co's railway - to give but a few. That which I have used is the one most commonly appearing in official documents and the one which most accurately describes the line at its fullest extent.

Similar problems of nomenclature occur with the variations during the time-span of the book in the spelling of place names. For example, Yarde has gained an 'e', Bury Moor was sometimes spelt Berry and Moor often appears in the plural, while some names of two words are now written as one or vice versa. In an attempt to be consistent, rather than confusing, I have endeavoured to use the modern spelling as used by the Ordnance Survey and trust that my readers will forgive me if this still differs from local usage.

It should also be mentioned that although not legally authorised as a light railway the T&MR is still correctly described as such, both today and in contemporary literature. It was built, maintained and operated to a lesser and more economical standard than the Board of Trade expected for a main line railway and therefore was, *de facto*, a light railway. No such doubts exist for the NDCJLR for it had a Light Railway Order to state that it was, and no matter whether it was built as economically as possible or simply operated thereafter it was, *de jure*, a light railway.

CHAPTER ONE
THE BEGINNINGS OF AN INDUSTRY

The closeness of Bideford to the river and to the sea must be readily apparent to the most casual visitor but few can realise how economically close the town was three hundred years ago. Nowadays a ship can still be seen from time to time loading clay at Bideford Quay but in the seventeenth century Bideford was one of the largest ports in Britain, only London and Topsham sending out more ships in 1699. Sir Richard Grenville was Lord of the Manor of Bideford and inevitably much of the traffic was with the British Colonies of North America, Bideford and Barnstaple becoming for fifty years the major tobacco ports.

This vigorous trans-Atlantic trade had considerable benefits for the potteries of Bideford, Barnstaple and, it seems, Torrington. The growing colonies provided a ready market for the local earthenware, a much greater market than they would otherwise have enjoyed. The potteries had come into being due to the proximity of clay deposits, in particular red clay at Fremington, which provided the raw materials for such products as ovens and harvest jugs. Items such as the latter were decorated with a white slip of pipe-clay, the white clays being found at Bideford itself, Wear Gifford and Marland, although the last named deposits were probably too remote to be worth the transport when used in such small quantities.

Possibly it was the connection with tobacco and the growing habit of smoking, founded by Sir Walter Raleigh, that gave the initial impetus to the North Devon clay workings. As the habit spread so did the craft of pipe-making, and with it the demand for white-firing clay - hence 'pipe-clay'. North Devon seems to have answered the initial demand, Bideford exporting clay to Bristol, Chester, Gloucester and other places in the 1690s.

Quite possibly the Staffordshire potters became aware of the properties of pipe-clay; suffice it to say that they needed a clay that produced a white-bodied product. South Devon clays fire in the kiln to a whiter shade than the North Devon clays but Wedgwood is said to have obtained clay from a pit near Meeth and also from Marland, and the Reverend John Swete said he saw Wedgwood's men in 1796 making test borings on Petrockstow moor. The clay is not used on its own for pottery, of course, but as part of a mixture which may include ball clays of various grades, china clay, ground flints and calcined bones.

There are several deposits of clay in North Devon, in the Fremington, Barnstaple and Bideford areas, for example, but it is the vast deposits of Marland and Meeth occupying a basin over four miles long that concerns this story for it is here that the important commercial exploitation has been. The only

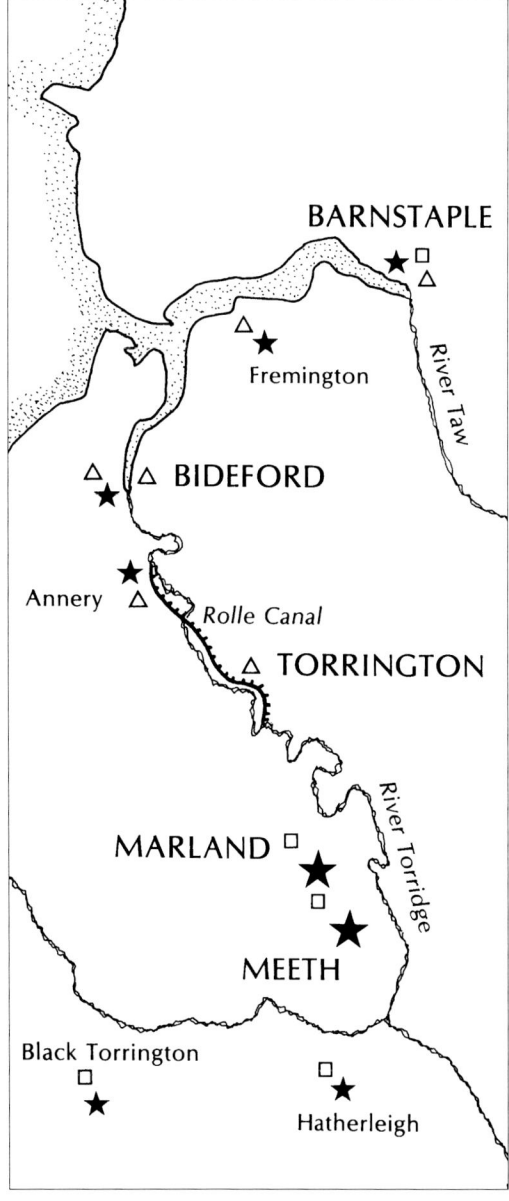

CLAY DEPOSITS
OF NORTH DEVON
★ Clay deposits
△ Potteries
□ Brick and/or tile works

comparable deposits, in extent and in quality, are in the Bovey basin in South Devon, and in Purbeck, Dorset. These were both much better placed for transport, being nearer the sea, and after the initial lead of North Devon, developments at these places overtook it in the first half of the eighteenth century.

The clay was deposited in the beds many millions of years ago by alluvial means. The Petrockstow Basin is on the line of a fault that crosses Devon from north-west to south-east and was once an ancient lake or river. From high ground to the east, south and west fine particles from weathered rocks were carried through the basin and in times of flood were deposited around the perimeter. Over the years the deposits increased in depth and were compacted to form the clays we now know. They are patchily deposited and sometimes contaminated with other things also brought down the river, such as iron staining or rotting vegetation. Whilst the former taints the clay, the latter, strangely, enhances it for the carbon that remains in black clay burns off in firing to give a white pottery. The depth of the sedimentary deposits varies; at the centre it is nearly 2,000 feet (661m) deep but the better clays are in thinner beds.

In the modern world the uses of ball clay extend well beyond ordinary pottery into vitreous china for sanitary-ware and into refractory materials. Its qualities as an inert filler found uses in animal feedstuffs, fertilisers, paint, rubber and plastics, so ensuring an increasing demand. But it is a naturally occurring mineral and despite modern science its idiosyncrasies, some of which are mentioned above, ensure that its extraction is still a skilled job, relying on the person in the pit and his knowledge and experience to maintain an even quality. As one hundred years ago, or two hundred years ago, apart from drying and blending, the clay that is sold is exactly what has been dug out of the ground.

Just when the Marland clays were first used is by no means clear but Polwhele in 1797 refers to large quantities of clay being dug in the area, perhaps the results of Wedgwood's explorations. By 1822, however, Lysons reported that the pits in Petersmarland and Petrockstow had not been worked for nearly 20 years and this may have been due to competition from the South Devon workings, which had considerable transport advantage by then. A filip for North Devon must have been the opening of the Rolle Canal in 1827 from Annery, up-river from Bideford, to Torrington which brought some improvement in accessibility for Marland clays.

The 1840 Tithe Map of Petersmarland parish shows no clay workings although two fields close to the village are named as Brickmoor and Brick Field, indicating at least a local use. When the 1845 Bideford & Tavistock Railway was surveyed, passing through Clay Moor, George Braginton was one of the occupiers of this, the later site of the Marland works, which by then included claypits and a brick-kiln. Braginton, the son of the steward of the Rolle Estate, was a banker and merchant and, significantly, was also a lessee of the Rolle Canal. He had managed it since about 1827 and from 1836 leased it. From about 1858 one of his partners in the Rolle Canal Company was Frederick Holwill.

Both Polwhele and Lysons mention the fine pipe-clay at Weare Gifford and the North Devon Pottery was established in 1849 by Henry Jones, from Staffordshire, later to be joined by John Goodman Maxwell of Bideford. There are accounts in the late 1850s of clay being brought from Marland and the pottery was described as an earthenware manufactory. By 1862 Braginton & Co. were running it and were making sanitary ware and sewer pipes with ball-clay from Marland. The clay would have been carried by pack-horse or cart to the canal at Taddiport, below Torrington, for shipment to Annery. Braginton became spectacularly bankrupt in 1865 and the canal returned to the Estate. It was superseded during 1871 by the construction of the standard gauge extension of the London & South Western Railway from Bideford to Torrington. The North Devon Pottery appears to have reverted to the Maxwell family, who owned the freehold.

In addition to the workings at Clay Moor during the 1850s Lord Clinton was extracting clay from Bury Moor, probably for local use, and later had his own brick and tile works nearby. At several places elsewhere in the district, Black Torrington and Hatherleigh for example, small deposits of clay were made use of for a local supply of bricks.

It would seem that although the North Devon clays enjoyed a wide market in the eighteenth, seventeenth and possibly even the sixteenth centuries, during the nineteenth century their use was stultified by the lack of good communications serving Marland and Meeth. Poor transport facilities have long been a hallmark of North Devon, and are still a problem today, but on 24 July 1872 Torrington was connected to the rest of Britain by rail. Perhaps it was the optimism generated by this event that started the developments at Marland that gave birth to the North Devon Clay Company.

CHAPTER TWO
THE MARLAND WORKS AND THE NORTH DEVON CLAY COMPANY

The Greening family were merchants at Bideford in the seventeenth century and were shipping pipe-clay from the port. From the second half of the century they owned land in both Petrockstow and Petersmarland parishes and it is quite feasible that clay came from here as well as the closer deposits at Wear Gifford. Clay Moor is also referred to as Greenings Moor. In 1768 Robert Wren, also of Bideford, married Sara Greening and the Greening lands moved into the Wren family. In 1840 the owners of Clay Moor were given as Robert, Josias and Thomas Wren and Robert Greening. By 1845 this had changed to Richard Greening and Robert Wren, but the land was occupied by George Braginton. Clay was certainly being extracted during the 1850s and 1860s.

A visitor to Clay Moor in July 1875 found a shaft nearly 80 feet deep, evidently exploratory, and it would seem that William Alderley Barton Wren, JP (1821-1893), son of Thomas and grandson of Robert, was assessing what was now his property. It was later said of him that he was 'a far seeing and enterprising man in commercial matters'. There is little documentary evidence of the clay workings at this period but fortunately some old bank pass-books survive which are quite revealing. Wren opened a 'Clay Account' with the National Provincial Bank of England at Bideford in April 1876 and would appear to have been trading from that time. Payments were being made to such as the Patent Brick Machine Co., Neath Abbey Co., Severn Carrying & Canal Co., Trimsaral Coal Co., London & South Western Railway, etc, and whilst we can only guess at their specific purpose there can be little doubt that the clay was being worked and shipped away.

By November 1877 the shaft had been filled in and clay was being dug from several pits. Certainly by the following year Wren had erected not only the kilns and buildings of the Marland Brick & Tile Works but cottages and stables also. Frederick Holwill (1823-1887), then aged 54, was manager. Holwill, a Torrington resident, was High Bailiff to the County Court and a coal merchant, and had been a partner in the Rolle Canal Company. Early in 1879 it was noted that the works was producing a 'remarkably hard tile'. To develop the works, on 12 December 1879 the Marland Brick & Clay

An extremely detailed view of a Marland clay pit about 1920 that still hangs in the office there. In the pit men have cleared a bench of clay ready for cutting and on the right the 'staircase' remains after balls have been removed. The skip awaits hauling to the surface by the engine in the shed at top-right to be emptied into the waiting train of wagons in the charge of PETER. On the far left is the pitwork of the pump and on the skyline, behind the overburden being removed, stands one of the workmen's transport vans.
NORTH DEVON CLAY CO.

This map, prepared for a sale of Clinton Estate properties in 1958, is an amalgam of 6 inch Ordnance Survey maps of different periods, hence the appearance of both British Railways and the Torrington & Marland Light Railway. At least a quarter of a century separated these two entities but it does show the Torrington & Marland at its fullest extent across the moors, and gives the locations of the various moors. The many branches serving mines can be seen but the original line, in the early 1880s, terminated in a simple short loop by the 'Old Clay Pit' roughly in the centre of this map.
BALL CLAY HERITAGE SOCIETY

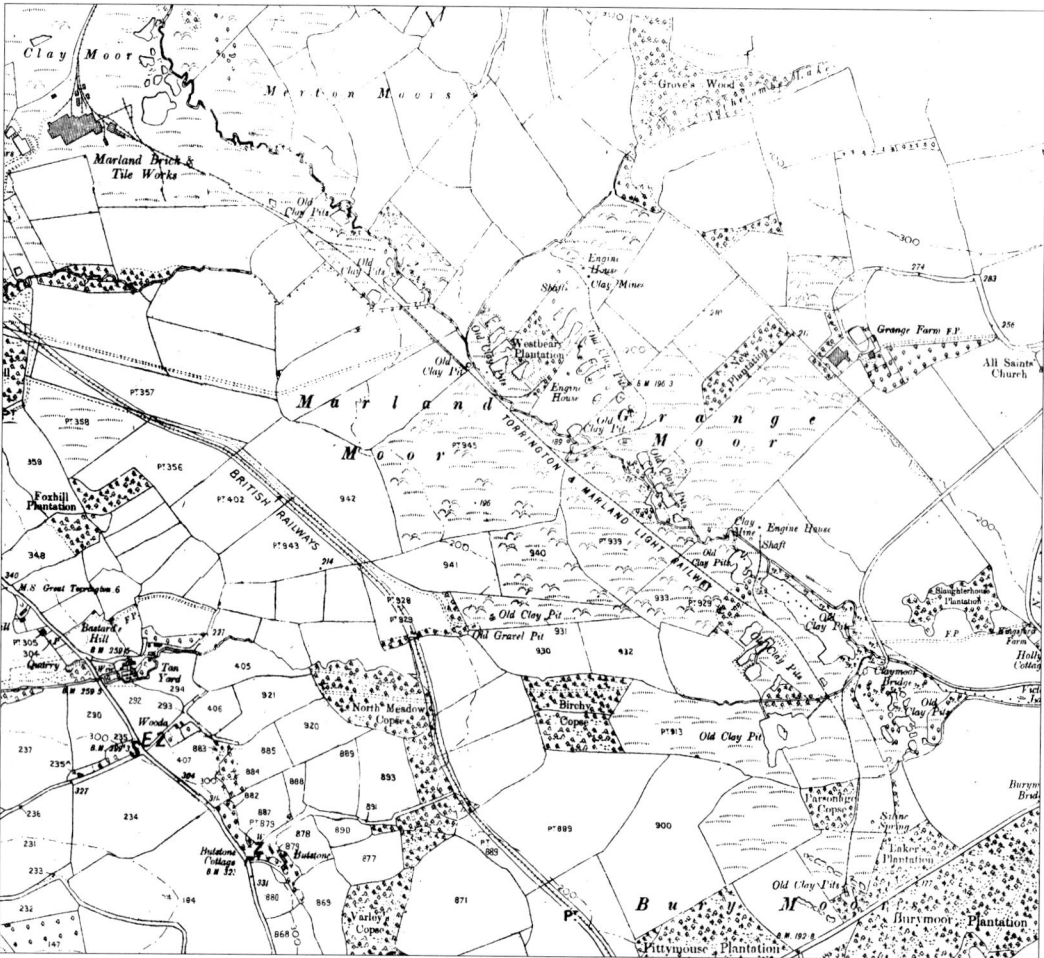

Works Limited was incorporated. It had an authorised capital of £25,000 in 100 shares and Wren had already agreed to lease the works and clay pits to the company for 60 years. He was to be paid £9,200, of which £5,000 was to be in 20 shares, and in addition was to receive £100 annual rent, plus royalties of 2s. for every 1,000 bricks, 9d. per ton of raw clay sold and 2½% of the sale price of terra cotta glazed bricks and other items. From these royalties the range of products the works was intended to produce is evident and an inventory of the machinery at this time shows how well equipped it was.

The inventory included one Galloway boiler, one 25hp steam engine with shafting and pulleys, two pans (for grinding), brick machines, presses, one traction engine and four waggons, two travelling cranes, three trolleys, six horses, a spring waggon, and much more in the way of small tools and equipment.

Investment on this scale meant an efficient means had to be found to export the products from the works and whilst the traction engine and waggons were an improvement on horses and carts it is no surprise to find that a railway was planned at an early date. Frederick Holwill was later credited with the idea and it is possible the whole venture may have been his conception, with Wren providing the capital. The story of the railway, its construction and operation, appears in the ensuing chapters. Suffice to say here that construction of the line, under the supervision of the noted engineer, J. B. Fell, began with the cutting of the first sod in May 1880 and the first train ran on New Year's Day 1881.

The North Devon Pottery, now owned by John Maxwell's widow, Eliza, and managed by Charles Kingsley Maxwell, was purchased in August 1880 for £1,687, presumably to eliminate competition, but perhaps also to obtain Charles Maxwell's expertise. In 1881 he was clay works manager at Marland and not long after the pottery was acquired by Candy & Co. of South Devon. 1,200 tons of clay a month were being sent away from the pits and the traffic necessitated the purchase of an additional locomotive in 1883. The same year Henry Holwill (1854-1925), Frederick's son, then aged 27, is noted as manager of the works.

However, at about this time a Mr J. W. Ludlam took over the works with a Mr J. M.

Limpus as his manager. It would seem from the bank pass-books of the Marland Brick & Clay Works Limited (this time with Fox Bros., Fowler & Co., Bankers, of Torrington) that the company traded on its own account from 1880 to 1883 judging by payments to the LSWR which would be for the shipment of bricks and clay. From May 1883 the fortnightly wages bill dropped by two-thirds and presumably this is when Ludlam took over the brickworks. Hugh Strong visited the works in 1889 and it is his account which tells us of Mr Ludlam.

Strong describes the works, its processes and equipment, in some detail. 75 men were employed and a variety of brick and tile products were made for sale all over England. In addition to the conventional brick the works sold paving and fire bricks and a large variety of architectural decoration in terra cotta. The latter department employed 25 men and their work had been sent to Brighton, Chelsea, Paignton and London's West End.

The brick process was not unusual. After arriving by rail from the pits the clay was taken by incline to the uppermost floor where it was rolled and ground, firstly by a pair of edge-runners and then in a pug-mill. The plastic clay was next extruded to shape and cut into individual bricks which were dried on top of the kiln before burning in it.

In addition to the machinery installed by Wren a 35hp engine was in use, and also a 20hp portable engine in the terra cotta department. A large circular continuous kiln was used for bricks and five other kilns for terra cotta. Production was about 25,000 bricks a day.

Strong did not visit the clay pits and this implies that Ludlam only occupied the works, for Kelly's Directory in 1889 mentions that Henry Holwill was still manager of the North Devon Clay Company. This firm, not a limited company, was also mentioned in 1881 and it seems that a division between clay extraction and brick manufacture had been made at an early date.

The Marland Brick & Clay Works Limited had been wound up in 1888; the company seems to have made a heavy loss each year of its short life. Wren was the major shareholder throughout the eight years and it would appear he was content to control the pits and railway, leaving the specialised brick and terra cotta manufacture to others. For eighteen months in 1887 and 1888 Wren was again trading in his own name, with another account at Fox Bros., Fowler & Co., presumably dealing in clay alone as Ludlam was still at the works.

In 1891 William Lawton, a brick manufacturer of Manchester, leased the works – the railway and clay pits being specifically excluded from the agreement. What happened to Ludlam is not known but in 1893 Limpus was manager of Candy & Co's works at Bovey Tracey. In 1892 Lawton surrendered his lease to another new company, the Marland North Devon Brick Company Limited. This was incorporated 8 September 1891, had a capital of £3,000 in £10 shares and most of the eight shareholders lived in Manchester. Eustace and Henry Holwill later had holdings in the company.

Wren's lease to the new company was dated 2 April 1892 and was for five years at £100 per annum rental. Like Lawton's surrendered lease it only covered the brick works but Wren agreed to 'carry in his trucks on his light railway between the works and the station all clay and manufactured goods and all coal and materials required'. Obviously ease of transport was an important factor to the new company.

The North Devon Clay Company under the management of Frederick Holwill, and later Henry, seems to have looked after the clay pits,

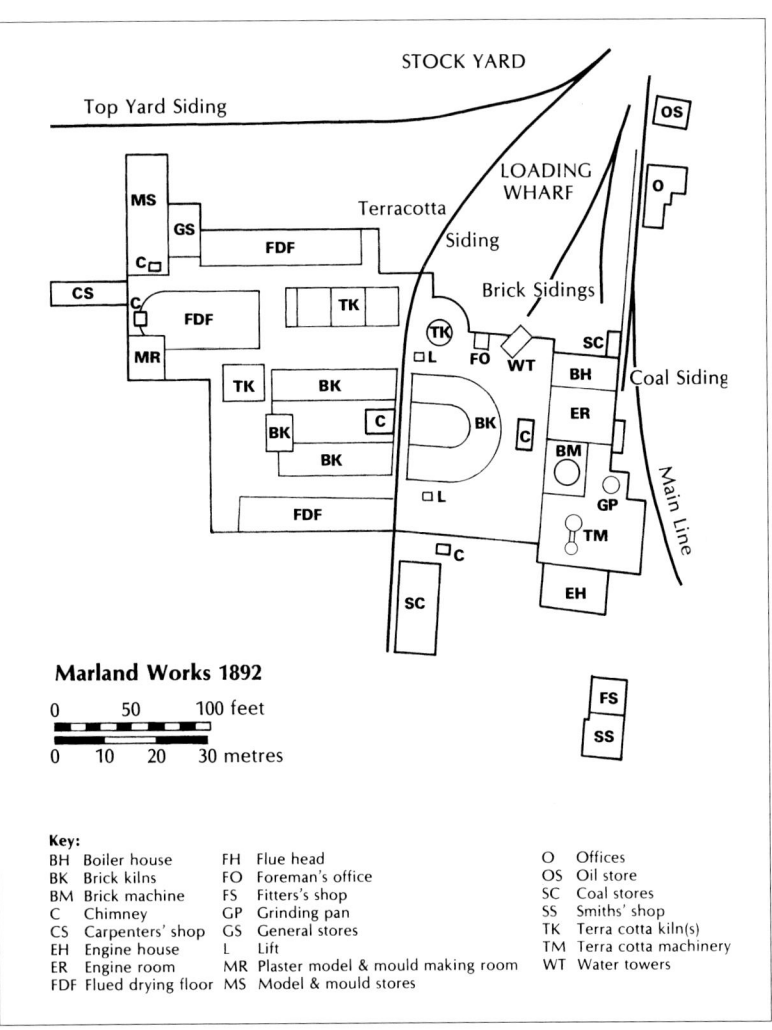

Marland Works 1892

Key:
BH Boiler house
BK Brick kilns
BM Brick machine
C Chimney
CS Carpenters' shop
EH Engine house
ER Engine room
FDF Flued drying floor
FH Flue head
FO Foreman's office
FS Fitters's shop
GP Grinding pan
GS General stores
L Lift
MR Plaster model & mould making room
MS Model & mould stores
O Offices
OS Oil store
SC Coal stores
SS Smiths' shop
TK Terra cotta kiln(s)
TM Terra cotta machinery
WT Water towers

Taken from a North Devon Clay Co. brochure of about 1900, this view shows the steep double incline for hauling clay out of the pit, the waiting train being loaded, headed by the vertical boiler locomotive, and another train headed by MARLAND on the left.
BALL CLAY HERITAGE SOCIETY

The basic tools of clay cutting. From left to right, a digger for undercutting the clay, a cutter for cutting down between the balls and a prodder, or 'prog', for propelling the balls across the bench. The bricks behind and the tiles below are products of the works.
M. J. MESSENGER

excavating the raw clay for sale to the brickworks or elsewhere. Clay was at first extracted from the ground north of the works but at an early date the land to the north-east and later the south-east was developed. In the five years to 1890 clay tonnage had doubled to over 10,000 tons a year and a report of 1892 stated that 20 acres had been worked and ten or twelve acres were being worked at that time. The open pits did not become exhausted but simply too deep to be kept satisfactorily free of water. The topsoil was first stripped off to expose the clay, which was then dug out by cutting into blocks of about eight inches (20cm) cube. The blocks were known as 'balls' and it is from these that the type of clay, and the industry, take their name. The balls were removed in rows across the floor of the pit, utilising special tools and their movement was lubricated by water. Some pits in 1892 were more than 30 feet (9m) deep and at about this time the first commercial shafts were sunk.

Several reports in the early 1890s give information as to the working and equipment of the company and a boiler insurance policy of 1891 is particularly valuable. As well as the four railway locomotives there were four other items of steam machinery in use. A Fowler traction engine of about 1875 was available for haulage and there was a portable engine by Brown & May of Devizes. Two vertical boiler machines completed the list; one was a winding engine built by the Albion Works, Rugeley, while the other, from a London works, does not have a purpose stated.

Lord Clinton had been working clay from his land at Bury Moor since at least the 1850s from shallow pits only 10 or 12 feet deep and in 1892 he agreed to lease to the NDCC the land beyond Clay Moor as far as Bury Moor. The railway had been extended to there in 1886, presumably with Lord Clinton's blessing. The expanding business made a re-arrangement of its administration necessary and in December 1892 Wren, now aged 71, agreed to lease to the brothers Henry and Eustace Holwill the entire works, railway and moors for a payment of £1,500 plus £650 yearly rent. A new company was to be formed, the North Devon Clay Company Limited, and in due course the properties were to be transferred by the Holwills to the new company. Many years later, in 1919, Henry Holwill wrote that Wren had been losing money heavily on the brickworks and was on the point of closing it down when he and Eustace stepped in. A few weeks later, on 26 January 1893, Wren died, leaving his estate to his slightly younger maiden sisters Elizabeth Sarah and Delitia Mary Wren.

The new company was incorporated on 20 May 1893 with an authorised capital of £20,000 in £10 shares. A quarter of this was to be shared between 17 people, presumably as the purchase price of the old (unincorporated) North Devon Clay Company. The two Holwills had 165 shares

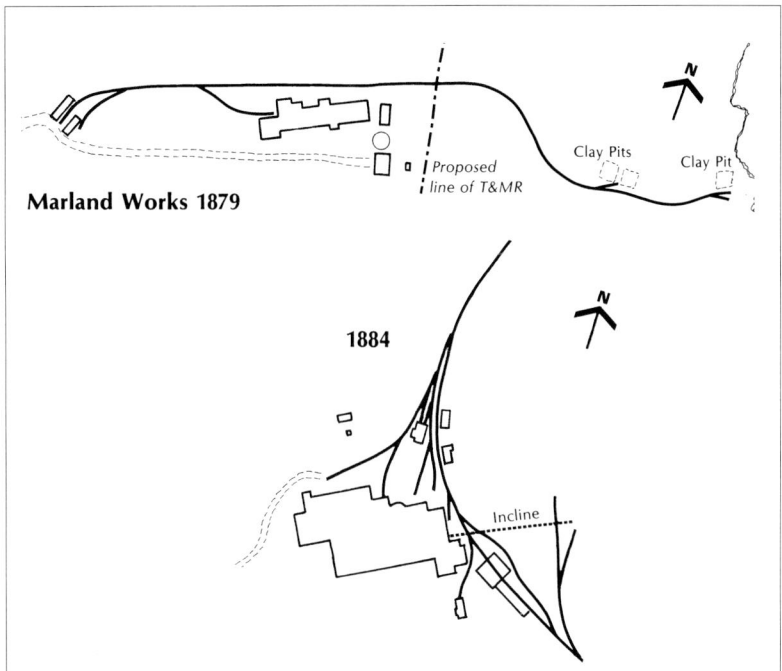

Removing overburden from a pit, prior to taking the next level of clay.
AUTHOR'S COLLECTION

Marland works. MARY is on the left and the engine shed in the centre. A train of tarpaulined wagons awaits departure. On the right are extensive stacks of earthenware drain pipes waiting shipment.
NORTH DEVON CLAY CO.

each and Eustace, who had been connected with the works for six years, was appointed Managing Director at a salary of £250 per annum plus 5% of the net profits. Henry, involved since 1878, became Works Manager on the same terms. In relation to the railway it is interesting to note that the company's stated objects included, as well as clay mining and manufacture, powers to act as general and agricultural dealers and as general carriers, amongst numerous other things. Eustace was said to have had 'considerable experience' in developing and working mineral properties.

The company's lease was subject, of course, to that already subsisting in favour of the Marland North Devon Brick Company Limited and no time was wasted in commencing negotiations to buy them out. Eventually agreement was reached and the lease surrendered to the NDCC in January 1894, in exchange for 27 shares. Negotiations should not have been too difficult as the brick company had not been making enough to pay their rent. It was wound up soon afterwards and the entire control of the brickworks, railway and clay pits was now in the hands of the North Devon Clay Company Limited.

Eustace Holwill 'retired' as Managing Director in June 1894 although he retained his connection with the company for a few years more, at least until the turn of the century, mainly in the capacity of London Agent. Why he should drop out after such a short time is not recorded but in the light of events 25 years later (see Chapter 9) some interesting speculations can be made. He had offices at Temple Chambers in London E.C. and these were initially the registered office of the company but this was soon transferred to 27 South Street, Torrington.

Some £225 had to be spent re-starting the brickworks and the next few years saw heavy expenditure on machinery and the railway but production of clay and bricks slowly increased.

A page of an advertising sheet illustrating the types of facing and moulded bricks produced in the 1890s.
NORTH DEVON CLAY CO.

14

The company traded in the name of The Marland Stoneware Brickworks and the bricks were particularly noted for their strength and imperviousness and found much use in lining strongrooms. They were also promoted on their acid resistance for paving and for engineering works, and as cream coloured facing bricks. Today they can be seen in many of the late-Victorian and Edwardian villas and houses of North Devon. The Lynton & Barnstaple Railway used many and the viaduct at Chelfham is a fine monument to Marland brick as well as to the erstwhile narrow gauge line it carried. Clay production reached 15,000 tons in 1900 and over 20,000 in 1905 while brick production in 1901 reached a peak of 2.8 million, a figure that was not to be exceeded for another 30 years.

The proposed Torrington & Okehampton Railway of 1895 threatened to take the route of the company's railway from Torrington and they at first opposed the proposals. However, nothing came of the plans although the company gained £1,000, the purchase deposit that the T&OR forfeited. (See Chapter 6 for full details of the T&OR fiasco.)

Following legal advice that the company would be in a better position to negotiate with the T&OR if they owned the freehold of their works the Misses Wren agreed to sell for £10,000 and in 1904 the ladies were issued with a debenture in this sum. Also gained by the NDCC was ownership of the plant and equipment and a long lease of the railway. In the same year the coal business of B. Read & Co. at Bury Moor was bought for the company to run themselves, but this investment merely cost £9 for the coal shed.

The management seem to have been very aware of the need to keep up with technological improvement, although in 1897 they decided a telephone was 'not advisable'. Henry Holwill was sent to Cornwall to see if anything could be learnt from the china clay industry of that county. By this time the open pits had mainly given way to shaft mining and some of the shafts were surprisingly deep. They were sunk into the clay at an angle of 75° from the horizontal and levelled out some 50 feet from the surface to reach an actual length of about 600 feet. Horizontal levels ran off the main shaft on either side to a distance of 60 to 90 feet. Small tramways were used underground and portable steam engines, or locomobiles, were used to haul the clay to surface. An oil engine was bought in 1910 but when it was used in place of a steam engine it was found that fumes got down the shaft.

Brick sales had declined since the turn of the century but clay sales were steadily increasing.

Clay was shipped from Fremington and Bideford and there was a useful trade with Europe and America, Liverpool being the usual shipping port for the latter destination. In 1898 the French barque *Henriette* had loaded 1,000 tons of ball clay at Bideford for Wilmington, Delaware, USA, and this was then said to be the largest cargo ever shipped from Bideford. Coastal shipping took the British traffic around to the Mersey where it was transferred to boats of the Trent & Mersey Canal or the Shropshire Union Canal for the rest of the journey to the Potteries.

The cramped heading at one of the NDCC mines with pneumatic shovels in use.
B. D. HUGHES

Some shafts were brick lined, using spoilt bricks from the works but some were bought in for the job.
NORTH DEVON CLAY CO.

Loading the SS Mari Eli at Fremington with 1,300 tons of ball clay. July 1934.
B. D. HUGHES COLLECTION

Transferring ball clay from main-line railway wagons to ships was a labourious business until mechanical grab cranes were introduced. This scene is probably at Fowey but similar procedures were used at Fremington.
B. D. HUGHES COLLECTION

The Great War dealt a severe blow to trade, and not just overseas trade as the U-boat threat had a severe impact on the coastal shipping that the company relied on. Clay production dropped by almost a half while brick production slumped alarmingly in 1916, ceasing altogether in 1918. Many of the clay workers were called up, or joined up, for the Army and a petrol driven machine was made at the works to cut clay, in place of the absent clay cutters. Henry Holwill had to seek a special licence for its fuel. With engineering raw materials diverted for the war effort the lack of spare parts made keeping the plant and machinery, including the railway, extremely difficult. Most of the German accounts were written off as bad debts in 1914, much to the detriment of the company's finances.

Not yet directly effecting the company but also held up by the War was Mr H. F. Stephens' proposed North Devon & Cornwall Junction Light Railway. First mooted in 1909, it had been delayed by lack of money, but when the War finished it was got under way again, as told in Chapter 7.

Business picked up rather slowly from 1919 and the arrears of maintenance and repairs to the railway and works were difficult to catch up with, the company's finances being at a low ebb. Surprisingly in 1921 the German accounts were honoured and the old pre-war debts were paid, enabling rejuvenation of many neglected assets. Henry Holwill again looked at the clay lands at Meeth but, as in 1895, decided that they were impossible to work economically without rail access. In 1920 the Meeth (North Devon) Clay Company was formed to work these and applied, unsuccessfully, to lease the then closed brickworks. (See Chapter 9 for an account of the Meeth works.) An undershot waterwheel, 30 feet diameter by 3 feet breast, was installed in 1919 to pump the clay pits.

The brickworks were got going again in 1923 but a union dispute of some sort caused production to cease almost immediately and it was not re-started until 1925 when the NDCJLR

The directors of the North Devon Clay Company outside their office in South Street, Torrington c.1930
A. P. HOLWILL

opened. From 1923 clay production averaged 30,000 tons a year while bricks, from 1925, averaged about two million. To finance the hoped-for growth in the twenties the share capital was increased by £30,000 in 1920. A similar increase six years later was funded by accumulated profits.

From late in the nineteenth century Hodges Bros., engineers of Exeter, later Marcus H. Hodges & Sons (Engineers) Ltd, had been playing a large role in the engineering needs of the works. They rebuilt some of the locomotives, installed the wagon tipper and did much of the routine engineering work for the plant, locomotives and rolling stock. This relationship lasted until at least the 1960s.

The depression at the beginning of the thirties saw a decline in clay tonnage setting in while brick sales, conversely, began to approach three million. During this time pneumatic shovels were introduced to replace the traditional tools. While these new shovels

One of the Fletcher Jennings locomotives with a train at the clay pits between the wars. Prominent are the tips of spoil or waste barrowed out from the shaft heads. The winding engines are to the right.
E. A. HOLWILL

A view of the clay pits taken about 1920, at the same time as those on pages 9 and 119. The two central figures also appear in that on page 9. On the left in the cloth cap is John Henry 'Jack' Holwill, who was pit foreman between the wars, whilst the gentleman in the bowler hat is possibly his father, Henry Holwill. The flimsy and ephemeral nature of both the shaft head frames and the track is readily apparent. The unsophisticated, but probably adequate, stub point is noteworthy.
NORTH DEVON CLAY CO.

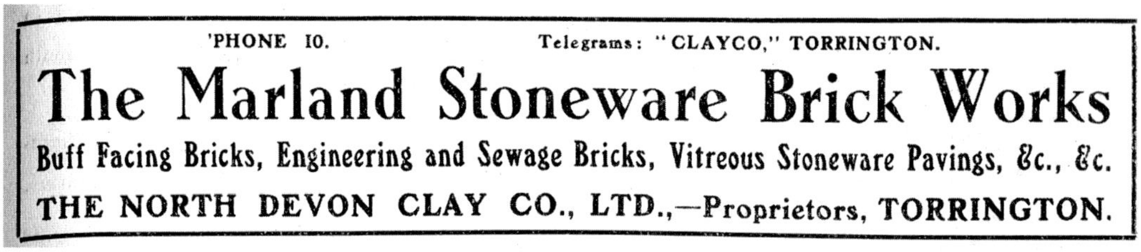
'PHONE 10. Telegrams: "CLAYCO," TORRINGTON.

The Marland Stoneware Brick Works

Buff Facing Bricks, Engineering and Sewage Bricks, Vitreous Stoneware Pavings, &c., &c.

THE NORTH DEVON CLAY CO., LTD.,—Proprietors, TORRINGTON.

Kelly's Directory 1926

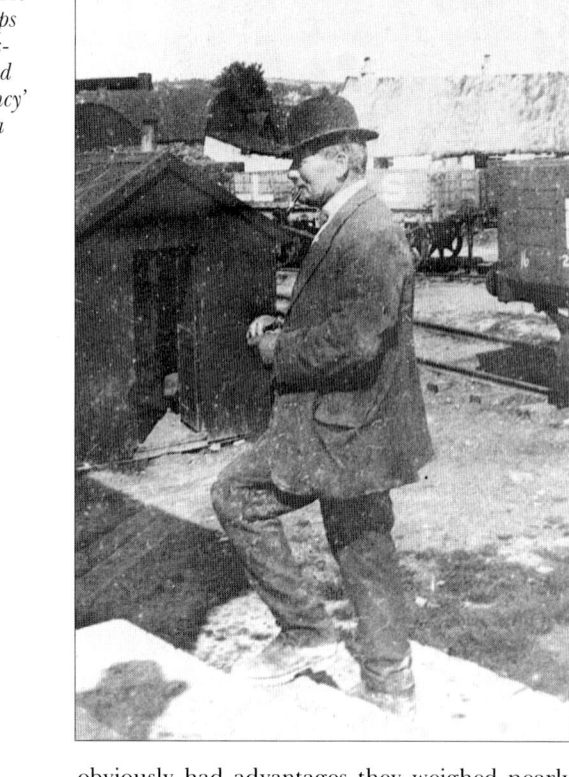

'Ganger' Martin was in charge of the works in the inter-war period. He is standing on the steps leading into the trans-shipment shed. Beyond the wagons is the 'fancy' shed where terra-cotta products were stored.
BEAFORD CENTRE

obviously had advantages they weighed nearly half a hundredweight (25kg) and in the cramped mines had to be lifted to head height for each cut of the clay. In the open pits mechanical diggers were used to dig out and transfer the clay to the narrow gauge trucks.

Electricity was introduced to the works and mines in 1936. The steam winches and belt driven ventilation fans were replaced by Holman electric hoists and electric fans, and in the following year Holman electric compressors were brought into use in the mines. Ventilating air was taken down the mines in six inch diameter galvanised tubes. Water was not a great problem, obviously when the clay nature of the ground is considered, and until 1937 was cleared by baling it into a tank lowered in the mine bucket. Thereafter compressed air pumps were used, initially to fill the tank but later to pump the water to surface.

Henry Holwill's nephew, Ernest Archibald Holwill (1905-1990), had joined the company in 1923 at the age of 18, working as a clerk. E. A. Holwill was the son of Henry's brother Alfred and had been brought up in Hampshire but regular holidays at Torrington evidently resulted in him joining the company. Henry died in 1925 and John Sillifant succeeded him as Manager until 1936 when he retired. E. A. Holwill now became General Manager and at the same time the office was moved to the works from Torrington. An indication of the depressed times the industry was seeing was the reduction in share capital in 1938 to £50,000 from £80,000.

The Second World War took away many of the young men who worked in the brickyard, for the forces or for munitions and foundry work elsewhere. Their places were taken by older men from the pits and mines but at the end of 1942 a large slip at the open pit cut supplies to the brickworks and it was decided to close the

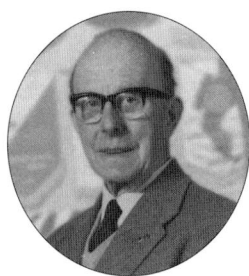

E. A. Holwill shortly after his retirement in 1973. He had long been involved in Torrington Borough Council and was Mayor in 1949. In 1970 he was made a Freeman of the Borough.
A. P. HOLWILL

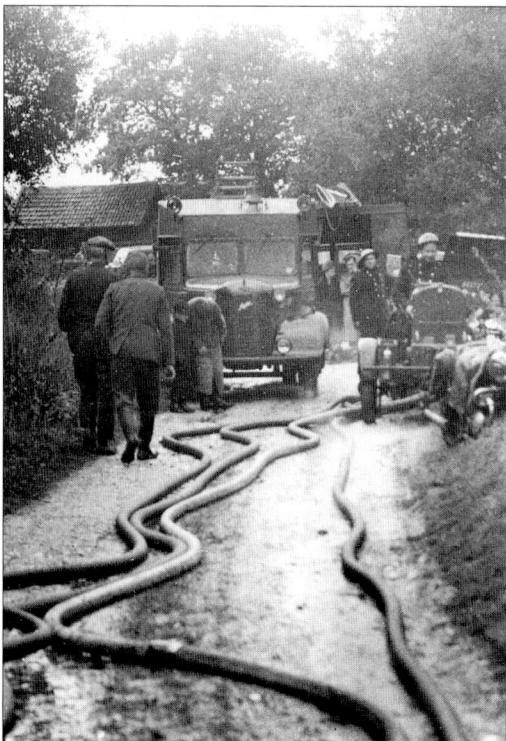

The wartime Auxiliary Fire Service attended when the works was destroyed in 1944.
NORTH DEVON CLAY CO.

Marland works, May 1940. On the far left a Jersey loco can be discerned, the weighbridge is on the left, the engine shed is central and on the far right the trans-shipment siding. Note the narrow/standard gauge crossing.
E. S. TONKS

latter. Large quantities of land drain pipes had been produced, many going to Winkleigh for construction of the airfield there, but the controlled price of bricks and the high price of the Nottingham steam coal that was needed for the kilns made continued operation of the brickworks uneconomic. It was requisitioned by the Ministry of Supply as a storage depot and E. A. Holwill became the Storage Officer, but in 1944 a fire destroyed it. Once again, the continental market for clay was closed, and the home market depressed, but the trans-Atlantic trade continued. 10,000-ton 'Liberty' ships called at Fowey to load up with china clay and ball clay for the United States and Canada as ballast for their return voyage.

A report on the mines made in 1948 reveals that the shafts varied in depth, according to the clay vein, from 20 to 100 feet, with gradients varying from 'moderate' to 1 in 3. The total length of each shaft was about 300 feet. 350 or 400 feet was the economical distance which would allow the miners to produce more clay to fill the bucket, actually a three-sided truck holding about one ton, by the time it had been hoisted to the surface and returned again. A team of six men were employed at each shaft; four underground and two on surface. From the furthest extent of the shaft the clay was worked out, if possible, to a distance of thirty feet on each side, working back. Each team had a daily allotment of clay to extract, known as a 'hag', and once that was done they could go home. This amounted to some 38 bucketfuls but the system for tallying this was open to abuse. The distance from the office no doubt helped this, so an additional weigh-bridge was installed on the moor between the pits and works to weigh all production; clay and waste. No attempt was made to revive the brickworks after the war and the site was levelled to provide the foundations of the present works, although the area continued to be known as the brickyard.

The 1960s were to see considerable change in the North Devon Clay Company's workings. In 1962 the company had co-operated in a

Test boring for clay prior to sinking a shaft. Marland in the 1950s.
BALL CLAY HERITAGE SOCIETY

In the 1960s extraction moved towards opencast workings, although not very efficiently. The excavator, hired from Woollaways, loads the company's dump truck which transfers the clay to an incline skip which in turn fills a railway wagon.
NORTH DEVON CLAY CO.

marketing scheme with Watts Blake Bearne & Co. Ltd., the major South Devon producer of ball clay. In 1967 a major stake in the share capital was taken by WBB and the following year the North Devon company became a wholly-owned subsidiary of the South Devon company. Technological change followed. There had already been a move to open working in pits where 10cwt (0.5 tonne) dumpers were loaded by hired JCB shovels and tipped into railway trucks. In 1969 underground mining ceased and by November 1970 road systems connecting the works and pits enabled the three-feet gauge railway to be dispensed with. Rubber tyred transport took over - diggers, dumpers and lorries the agents of the revolution - and the old order was swept away.

In 1967 94 men raised 35,000 tons of ball clay from nine mines and one small pit but by 1980 35 men produced 100,000 tons from two big pits, Westbeare and Courtmoor. 75% was exported to many countries ranging from France and Greece to the United States, India and New Zealand, to customers in the electroporcelain, tableware, sanitaryware and tile industries.

Despite the technological advances the skill of the digger driver is still necessary to supplement the laboratory analysis. Clay comes in differing qualities and is subject to adulteration with materials such as sand, lignite, iron pyrites and siderite, in varying quantities. The four basic types of clay - still using traditional names '120', '110', 'brokes' and 'darks' - are further broken down into 17 selections. The selection is made at the quarry face and taken to the appropriate storage bay. Dump trucks now (2007) carry 20 tonnes and the workforce totals just 20, managed from South Devon.

The scale of the operation is now larger than it has ever been. The spine between Courtmoor and Westbeare is steadily being removed to form one large quarry 800m by 400m. Whilst the deposits are some 100m in depth the workings are actually around 25m. Courtmoor is now being back-filled with waste and the working will move north into Merton Moors eventually. Old shafts are frequently intercepted.

In November 2006 the largest ever shipment, to date, was made from Bideford. Over three days 8,600 tons of ball was loaded on

A Ruston diesel stands with a train in one of the storage sheds, in the 1960s.
AUTHOR'S COLLECTION

to three ships of the largest size that could reach Bideford Quay. They were the *MV Celtic Freedom*, the *MV Casablanca* and the *MV Konnstentin*.

WBB itself has been acquired by a Belgian company, SRC Sibelco, but retains its identity and now trades as WBB Minerals. Production in 2006 was in excess of 500,000 tonnes, but not all is of saleable quality. Waste is inevitable but great efforts are made to maximise the yield. A filter press has recently been installed to extract clay from deposits in settlement ponds. 40% of sales go to the South Devon works to blend with their clays to improve the quality, 20% goes to UK markets and the remaining 40% is exported. The majority goes via Bideford, taking 60 lorry-loads a day to load a ship, and some to Plymouth and Teignmouth. Most is now used for ceramics and sanitaryware, particularly tiles in Spain and bricks in Finland.

Clay being transferred to a shredder. This machine was based on a turnip chipper and built by Hodges. The wheels are from a Bren-gun carrier and between them are flanged wheels for manoeuvreing on rails.
NORTH DEVON CLAY CO.

Trans-shipment of clay from narrow gauge to standard was an efficient operation in the purpose built split-level shed.
NORTH DEVON CLAY CO.

Seeking out the mine shafts was an adventure. These ramshackle structures were lost in the undergrowth on Marland Moor and were certainly picturesque. May 1968.
M. J. MESSENGER

The angle of the shaft incline dropping to the right can be clearly seen while the cable goes left to the winder, out of site. The wagons that took the clay also brought pit props. May 1968.
M. J. MESSENGER

A narrower gauge track also ran from the pit head to remove spoil and waste clay. May 1968.
M. J. MESSENGER

Ruston 518187 propels a train of clay away from a shaft head. May 1968. M. J. MESSENGER

CHAPTER THREE
THE TORRINGTON & MARLAND RAILWAY

W. A. B. Wren, owner of the Marland clayworks, and his manager, Frederick Holwill, clearly saw efficient transport as the key to the success of their enterprise because the building of a rail connection to Torrington was high in their order of priorities.

The survey of a route was made by July 1879 and showed two or three alternative routes, probably to accommodate different landowners. W. A. B. Wren soon set about gaining the consent of the various landowners along the path of his proposed railway and encountered little difficulty. The principal landowners were J. E. Moore Stevens and Lord Clinton and all seemed to be of the opinion the railway would be a useful thing. Only nominal rents were charged for land so that the annual rents for the entire length of the railway totalled less than £25. Torrington Town Council, the Highway Board and the Torrington commoners also agreed and raised no objections.

J. B. Fell had made the survey and he was formally appointed engineer in June 1880. He was to be paid 5% of the expenditure plus £105 in cash for 'extras' and of the payment £500 was to be in shares of the Marland Brick & Clay Works Limited.

In May MB&CW had awarded the contract for construction of the railway to the Green Odd Railway & General Contracting Company Limited, who had tendered £10,580, and the agreement, dated 1 May 1880, provided for construction to be commenced within one month and to be completed within seven. This company was owned by J. B. Fell and his sons and took its unusual name from the village of Greenodd in Cumbria, the family home of the Fells.

John Barraclough Fell, then 65 years of age, had had a distinguished career building railways in many parts of the world. Whilst being responsible for numerous conventional railways, he became particularly noted for mountain railways, having built the world's first such railway over the Mont Cenis Pass between France and Italy. The Snaefell Mountain Railway in the Isle of Man still makes, in part, use of his patent centre-rail system. Later his interests turned to monorails and subsequently to narrow-gauge and light railways, although much of Fell's work was in the realm of theoretical engineering and saw little practical application. Interesting though these matters are they are not relevant to the Torrington & Marland Railway, apart from one particular patented idea that Fell was to use the line to demonstrate.

The Marland line was specifically designed to be a cheap and economical railway that was still capable of handling efficiently the traffic it was required to carry. It was to be built to three-feet gauge, as this enabled considerable savings to be made in earthworks, and single track, with sidings to be provided where traffic demanded. No signalling or elaborate stations were planned and by gaining the consent of all landowners *en route* the expense of an Act of Parliament was avoided. A conventional standard-gauge line would have cost two to four times as much but would have served the district little better, if not worse because of the additional costs. There were a number of light railway theorists about at this end of the nineteenth century and Fell's ideas were much in line. One feature that was distinctive, however, was the use of wooden viaducts in lieu of embankments and bridges,

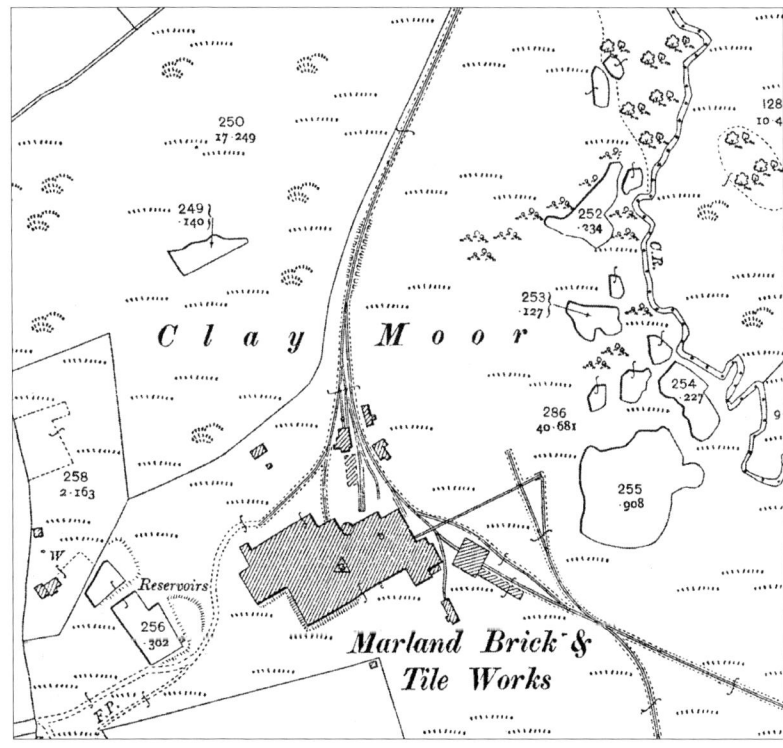

Marland works from the Ordnance Survey of 1906.

and this was the subject of patents taken out by Fell. These interesting structures are examined in a separate chapter.

The first sod of the railway was cut close to Torrington station with a small ceremony on Wednesday 26 May 1880 by Mrs Mary Fell, junior, newly wed to J. B. Fell's son, George Noble Fell. As soon as the party adjourned to Warren House, where the Fells were staying, a number of navvies commenced work. A field was taken over at Staple Farm, close to the London & South Western Railway (LSWR) station, where a steam saw mill was set up. Construction proceeded apace and by the end of June it was reported that nearly a mile of trackbed at the Marland end was ready for the permanent way. One of the biggest jobs was to be the sixty-feet long tunnel underneath the turnpike road (now the A386) immediately outside Torrington station and this was to take nearly four months. One suspects it was a cut-and-cover tunnel. Certainly the biggest single job was the viaduct across the River Torridge and the local populace watched its progress with some scepticism, doubting that such a flimsy and frail looking structure could carry a locomotive and train.

As soon as the permanent way was down it was made use of by the contractors, and one of the few recorded accidents took place at this time. John Newcombe and several other employees of the contractors were riding down the railway on a 'trolley', no doubt by gravity, when he fell off. One of the wheels ran over him, breaking a leg and injuring a hand. By early December the line's first engine, *Mary*, had arrived and was pressed into use by Fell's men.

It reflects greatly on Fell's organisation, and perhaps also on his novel method of construction, that the line was completed on schedule. It had cost £15,000; nearly half as much again as the estimate. Although only 6¼ miles (10km) long it included no less than ten timber structures, varying from small bridges to the 316 yard (287m) long Torridge Viaduct. The first train, carrying bricks and clay to Torrington, ran on New Year's Day 1881 and Wednesday 19 January was fixed as the date for the formal opening ceremony. In the event a snowstorm caused this to be cancelled and on 5 February, at Mr Fell's invitation, a party of the Press travelled over the line. With them were the Mayors of Torrington and Barnstaple and local landowners, and after touring the works at Marland the party returned to Torrington where they were entertained at the Globe Hotel to 'a sumptuous dinner'. Afterwards Fell spoke at length on the railway and on his theories for light railways generally.

Perhaps the best impression of the new railway, particularly as it appeared to the local people, can be gained from the account of this visit that appeared in the *Bideford Weekly Gazette*:

At 12 o'clock precisely the whistle blew, and the small party were taken at once gently through a short tunnel, some of them raising a faint cheer. On emerging, however, and getting on to the slender looking bridge, right above the river Torridge, and from thence on to a timber viaduct, 266 [sic] yards in length, and forty feet in height, the feeling of jollity suddenly changed to one of wonder and tremulation - wonder that engineering skill could devise so light a structure combined with safety, and tremulation lest the one thought uppermost in the minds of all should be realised. A looker-on from the common above afterwards informed us that the movement of the train across the viaduct as he looked down upon it presented the appearance of a party of children being conveyed across a toy bridge in perambulators. Even the lazy cattle which had been before quietly grazing in the meadow by the river were startled at this new intrusion upon their quietude, and went frisking along in all sorts of attitudes to seek shelter in the hedge beyond. As however, steam was put on, and we rattled along on what was, comparatively speaking, terra firma, round the thickly wooded slopes of Penclive [sic] Valley, reassurance returned, only to leave us again on finding ourselves on a viaduct crossing a narrow gorge dividing a most picturesque and well studded wood. In fact the scenery through which the line passes from beginning to end is of such a character as can rarely be seen from any railway in England. Over viaducts (ten in number) with perfectly upright supports, through the centre of woods, up steep gradients, over boggy moors, then falling on a gradient of one in thirty, all the while making some pretty sharp curves, and all of this on a line not 6½ miles in length is a kind of travelling such as Devonshire people are unaccustomed to in their own county. It was possibly this fact that struck terror to the hearts of some of the more innocent and less experienced of the party, but by-and-by noticing that Mr Fell himself was at the front, and that the engine was under the complete control of the driver, noticing also that on each viaduct there was a substantial guard rail, and then recollecting, too that Mont Cenis had been conquered by this same skillful engineer with his light railway, all qualms died away, and the return journey found us devoting more attention to the scenery above and below than to the distance we were from mother earth, and discussing the probabilities of extending this most useful piece of railway on to Hatherleigh, and from there on to Sampford Courtenay, there joining the Okehampton line.

The first experiences of travelling over a light railway may be unpleasant, but everyone saw that the element of complete safety was combined with the lightness and the cheapness of a railway of this kind.

Fell evidently intended the Torrington & Marland Railway to be an example of his theories and a demonstration line. When the first locomotive was ordered from Black, Hawthorn in June 1880 it was specified that she was 'to be a first class job, well fitted and finished, to pass Government inspection'. As a private railway the Torrington & Marland had no need for a 'Government inspection' by the Board of Trade Railway Department, so Fell was intent on other people taking an interest.

The first such interest was on 15 February 1882. Mr Fung Yee, Secretary of the Chinese Legation in London, complete with pigtail and traditional Chinese attire, became the first Chinese man to visit the town, and caused no small stir locally. His purpose was to inspect Fell's railway as the Chinese Government was considering similar light railways to open up their country. The Japanese Ambassador was also expected for the same reason but he was prevented from attending. Accompanying Fung Yee was a Major Grover, RE, of the War Office,

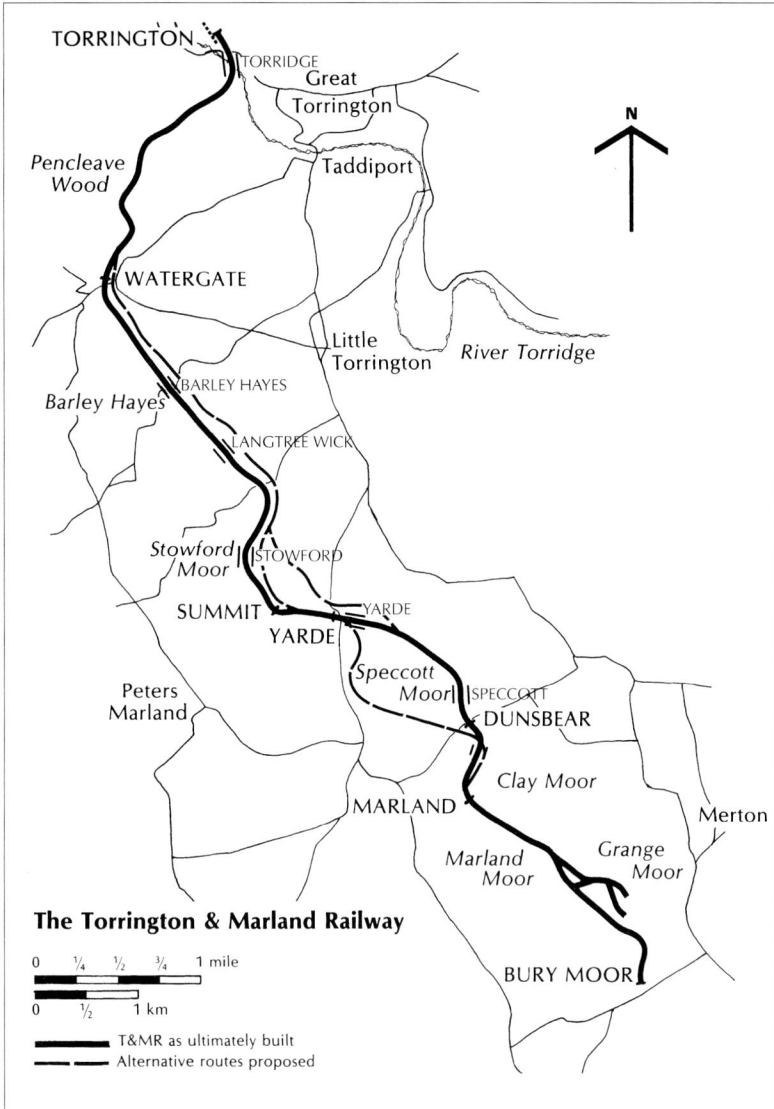

who had inspected Fell's earlier 18-inch gauge line at Aldershot and who came to Marland to see the improvements incorporated in the three-feet gauge railway. Other people also came to see the railway but what results accrued for Fell in the long term are unknown.

Immediately the line opened the local highways board noted the unfinished state of the roads at level crossings and at Watergate in particular only single gates were installed instead of the agreed double gates. The Rolle Estate also sought increased headroom under the bridge over the Rolle Road, the former canal bed, from 14 feet to 16 feet. Unwelcome attention to the railway came in May 1881 when 14-year old Samuel Johns, son of a farm labourer living at Stowford Moor, was prosecuted for letting off the brakes of wagons left at Summit. They ran for a mile, smashing gates and doing five pounds worth of damage.

NORTH DEVON CLAY

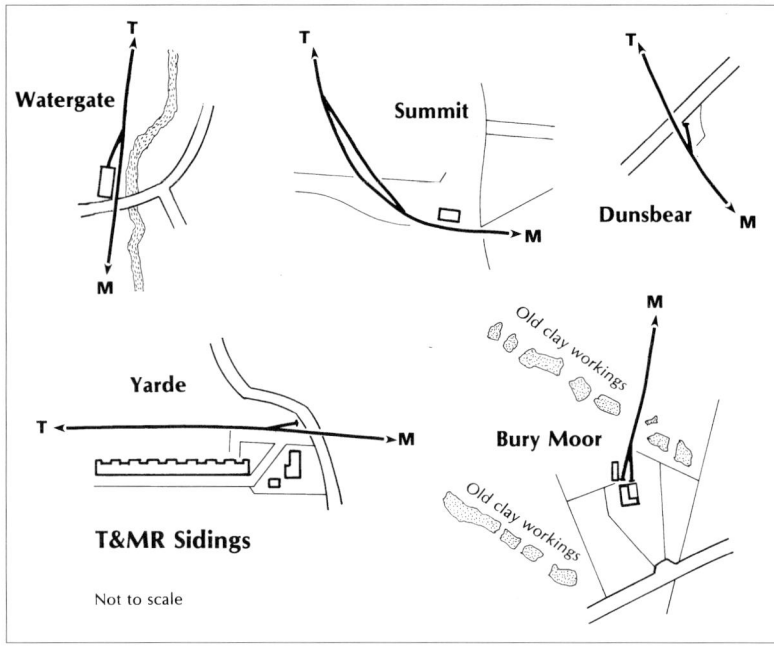

A rather gloomy view of AVONSIDE at Torrington with several features of interest. What the casks carried is not known but the wagon appears specially adapted for them. Beneath the train can be seen the turntable pit that existed here for a time.
FRANK JONES COLLECTION

A condition that had been written into the various leases and agreements that Wren made with the landowners along the line of the railway was that it would be available to carry the goods and farm produce of the landowners and their tenants. To this end sidings were to be laid where necessary and they were soon installed at Watergate, Yarde and Dunsbear. In addition trucks would be loaded and unloaded anywhere convenient on the mainline. How much was charged for this is not known; some agreements quote a maximum figure of 6d per ton per mile while another gives 1d per ton per mile. Consistent figures for this traffic are not available but in 1881 it was estimated at 3,000 tons and 2,500 tons would be a good average for most years, although in 1909 it was stated to be 5,000 tons. The only traffics that could not be handled were livestock and timber as there were no wagons suitable but there was a demand, albeit unsatisfied. From the start therefore the line was intended to be not merely a private company railway but of real service to the local community.

People living to the south of Petersmarland, beyond the railway, were very impressed by it and rumour was soon circulating that it was to be extended to Hatherleigh and Black Torrington, and even to Sampford Courtenay, on the LSWR line to Okehampton. Whether such an extension was seriously considered is not known but it would of been of little advantage to the company and Wren. The line was extended to Bury Moor in 1886, to the limit of land controlled by the company.

In 1879 there was about a quarter of a mile (0.5km) of railway connecting the pits and works but no details of this survive at all. It was probably worked by horse- or man-power and the first recorded locomotive to arrive at Marland was the 0-6-0ST *Mary*. She was a large locomotive, intended for the run to Torrington, and the lines bringing in clay from the pits were probably worked as before. However, growing business caused a smaller locomotive named *Tudor* to be hired in March 1883 and this could only have been for use in the pits and works. A second 'main-line' locomotive, *Marland*, was bought in 1883.

The Fells retained their connection with the district and with the clay company and railway for some time afterwards. Sadly G. N. Fell's wife, Mary Elizabeth, who dug the first sod, died just a few months later, aged only 25, before the line was even open. However, in 1888 he married Sarah Honoria Hole, of Torrington. In 1893 he was one of the subscribers and first shareholders of the newly formed North Devon Clay Company Ltd and was formally appointed consulting engineer. He advised the company on railway and engineering matters for many years. George Fell was also involved in other local railway proposals but none came to fruition.

There are few clues to what volumes of company traffic were carried at this time. 12,000 tons of clay, bricks and coal were estimated in 1881 but this seems a little high in view of later figures. Some figures are available from 1886 onwards but it is not clear if these are for sales or production, or if the clay tonnages include that part subsequently made into bricks. It would be reasonable, though, to estimate a figure of 10,000 tons annually by the end of the 1880s.

Both J. W. Ludlam and William Lawton, as lessees of the brickworks, had use of, but not control of, the railway for their transport needs. Lawton's terms were 4s 6d per truck from Marland to Torrington and 2s 6d in the reverse direction. The very much lower rate for return traffic probably reflects the fact that most traffic was to Torrington and the trucks had to come back anyway. Lawton was permitted three tons per truck and a maximum of 120 truck loads. No period is specified for the latter but it must have been per week - three trips a day.

Facilities at Torrington were very simple. A single siding ran into the goods yard, by courtesy of the LSWR, opposite the passenger station, and the layout was completed with a short run-round loop between the tunnel and the viaduct. There is a reference to a turntable at Torrington and photographic evidence bears this out, on one side of the run-round loop, but it was shortlived. Henry Holwill later rented a shed and coal store here from the LSWR. Elsewhere, apart from the three sidings at Watergate, Yarde and Dunsbear, the only other installation outside the works and pits was a loop at the summit of the line at Yarde, where there was a shed erected at Lord Rolle's request for goods and merchandise. At the works sidings served the stockyards, where the finished products were stored, and the coal yards for the boilers of the brickworks. There is a suggestion on an early map of a turntable at the engine shed but, like that at Torrington, it does not appear to have lasted long. From the works the line continued to various clay pits, as required, and after 1886 to Bury Moor. A team of six 'packers' or platelayers maintained the line.

The method of working probably varied little during the lifetime of the railway and at the end the line was worked in two sections, divided at the summit loop. Two short trains of four full wagons each would be worked to Summit from the works to be made up into a train of eight for the remainder of the trip to Torrington. Locomotives would be exchanged at Summit; that from the works returning with empties while that for the Torrington side, stabled overnight in the tunnel, having brought the empties up, took the full train down to the main-line interchange. There was no signalling as such, or timetable, and trains were controlled by the needs of the works, but at the very least the workmen's train had to run regularly morning and afternoon. The first train left Torrington at 6.25 each morning with the clayworkers, returning with a load of clay about 9am. Another trip, if required, was made at about 10am, whilst a third in mid-afternoon was able to return at 6pm with the men. On Saturdays the workmen returned at midday. Some 100 tons of clay a day could be handled in this way. Latterly *Mary* or *Marland* would work from the works and *Avonside* was based at Torrington.

NORTH DEVON HERALD, 20 May 1886.

As clay pits became too deep to work fresh pits were opened and the railway extended to serve these. In 1884 it ran for half a mile (1km) to the south-east of the works but within a couple of years it reached south-east to Bury Moor where a small depot of two sidings for public traffic was established, opening by May 1886. The extension was not only for the purpose of opening up the new deposits of clay but also to provide rail facilities for Lord Clinton's estate at Heanton Satchville and the neighbourhood. Henry Holwill advertised its availability in the local papers and a small coal depot was soon opened here. It was close to Lord Clinton's brick and tile works, across the road. A further mile was added to the route length of the railway by this extension.

In 1893 the North Devon Clay Company was incorporated into a limited liability company and because many company records survive our knowledge increases considerably from this time. A prospectus for the new company gives some useful information on the railway which was then 7½ miles (12km) long. There were four locomotives - 'two good six-wheel coupled' for the railway and two more for the clay works - and forty-nine wagons. There

A carriage account for public traffic; four tons of fertiliser to Bury Moor from Western Counties Agricultural Co-operative Association.

On 11 August 1899 the Devonshire Association visited Marland works and travelled on the railway, later reporting: 'On Friday the second visit of the Association to the charming and attractive district of Great Torrington was brought to a close by a delightful and instructive excursion to the works of the North Devon Clay Company at Marland. Mr Holwill, the manager of the works, had very kindly caused a considerable number of the clay trucks to be fitted with seats, and the party was thus enabled to travel from Torrington over the tiny railway, whose trestle bridge is so conspicuous a feature of the Torridge, through most charming woodland scenery to their destination. Except for occasional showers of ashes from the engine on the unprotected passengers, the journey was thoroughly enjoyed.' AUTHOR'S COLLECTION

A charming study at Summit loop where the train from Torrington waits to be taken on to the works by MARLAND, probably soon after the Great War. The young boy sitting at the far corner of the rear wagon is E. A. Holwill. Interestingly the party prefers to travel in an open wagon rather than the tram-car.
COLLECTION B. D. HUGHES

were also nine standard-gauge wagons on the LSWR. It was 'the only convenient means of carriage to the district used by residents for carriage of all kinds of goods. It naturally gives the monopoly of sale of coal, lime and manure.' In 1891 the railway had earned £550 from public traffic, a substantial contribution to the working expenses of £915. During the next few years receipts from public traffic were a little over £300 to set against railway wages of £600/700 per annum.

Tonnages of clay and brick carried on the railway increased slowly but steadily as the nineteenth century drew to a close and as it turned the need for another main-line locomotive became urgent. Second-hand engines were sought but eventually a new 0-6-0ST by the Avonside Engine Co. was bought. On average 25,000 tons were being carried each year.

An unfortunate accident happened on 20 September 1900. William Lethbridge and Henry Sanders were the driver and stoker, as the NDCC called firemen, on a locomotive travelling between the pits and works, and were giving a lift to a clay cutter called Laurence. Travelling at about 10 m.p.h. the locomotive derailed and threw the three men off. Lethbridge picked himself up, rather shaken, and found Sanders and Laurence both unconscious. The locomotive was on its wheels but off the rails and almost completely turned around. An axle was broken, so was the safety valve and the chimney was knocked off, suggesting that it had turned over. As no damage to a cab is mentioned the engine was probably *Peter*. Laurence sustained a head wound but Sanders did not regain consciousness and died in hospital five days later. The speed was not thought excessive but Henry Holwill admitted the track was not in the best condition as the clay ground made it impossible to keep the sleepers well packed. The inquest returned a verdict of accidental death on Henry Sanders.

Many of the clayminers and brickyard workers lived at Torrington or Yarde and travelled to work daily on the railway. The company were concerned enough for their safety to insure against accident. No doubt the local populace found the line useful also and one suspects it was an easy matter to obtain a lift on the mineral trains. In 1909 two former horse-tram cars were purchased for use as workmen's carriages and at this same time it was decided to try to restrict the numbers of illicit passengers. Drivers were instructed to take names of people where necessary.

31

This photograph appeared in THE LOCOMOTIVE in 1913. MARY brings the late afternoon train across the Torridge Viaduct. Behind the wagons are two shanties and one of the tramcars although some workmen still prefer to ride on the wagons.
JOHN ALSOP COLLECTION

MARY crossing the Torridge Viaduct with a train of empty wagons.
LOCOMOTIVE & GENERAL RAILWAY PHOTOGRAPHS

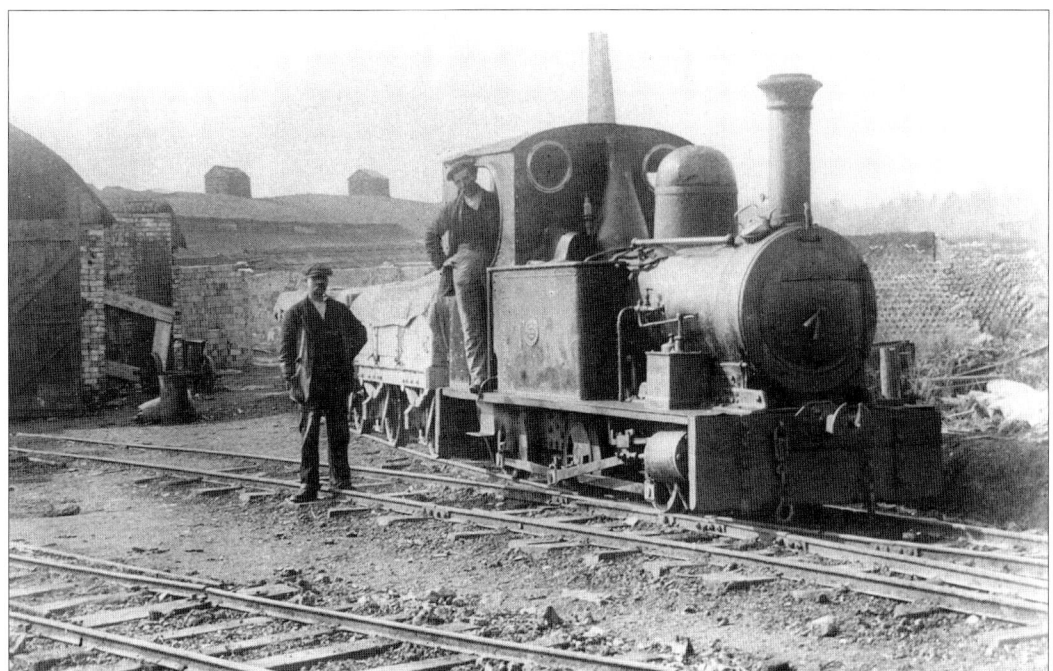

MARLAND with a loaded train in the stock yard at Marland works, about 1913. The engine shed door is on the left.
LOCOMOTIVE PUBLISHING CO.

One reason for this may have been the deteriorating state of the timber viaducts which seem to have been causing some concern. In 1912 it was noted that the Torridge Viaduct would need considerable repair during the summer. This was probably due to age but the increasing traffic could not have helped matters.

Second-hand three-foot gauge steam locomotives were not too common so the opportunity was taken to purchase three tank engines from Jersey in 1908, but it was some years before all were brought into use. The cost of working in 1911 was given as 1½d per ton mile, excluding management expenses.

The Great War had a considerable impact on the works and railway. The downturn in production was inevitably reflected in traffic carried although some extra was the carriage of pit-props, vital for the war effort, for a Bideford timber merchant. The lack of maintenance and repairs during this period meant that many of the locomotives were in a parlous state by the end of hostilities and Henry Holwill was very anxious lest a major breakdown would stop traffic altogether. Spare parts were simply not available and, for example, *Marland* had to have a new firebox of steel rather than copper and performance suffered accordingly. During 1920 Holwill was making numerous enquiries for new or second-hand three-feet gauge locomotives for the main line.

As things were getting back to normal, the North Devon & Cornwall Junction Light Railway showed signs of becoming a reality and this was to have major repercussions on the mineral railway. The new railway finally got the go-ahead in 1922 and the three years it took in building caused a great deal of disruption to the Torrington & Marland Railway.

It was part of the agreement with Colonel Stephens (as he now was) that Andersons, the contractors for the NDCJLR, should have the use of the Marland line for their works, although the clay traffic was always to have priority and the route was not to be severed. Andersons first looked over the route in June 1922 and did not seem to be aware of the agreement but in September Henry Holwill gave them the all clear to use the line, although he had reservations about the weight of the short wheelbase four-wheeled locomotives Andersons intended using. By December the contractor's traffic was heavier than the clay

PETER left soon after 1920, and this view is of particular interest as it shows a train of works-built wagons with long drop-side doors, confirming that such wagons were introduced well before the standard gauge reached the works. A stub point can be seen by the rear wagon.
TOM BARTLETT POSTCARD COLLECTION, BERRYNARBOR, EX34 9SE

NORTH DEVON CLAY

AVONSIDE backs on to its train at Torrington. This view is taken from the main road looking southwards with the Torridge Viaduct in the background. The turntable has been removed and the pit filled but the curve of the right-hand line reveals its location. COLLECTION H. C. CASSERLEY

company's and Holwill was claiming damage to the track. Andersons' agent, a Mr Cox, responded, probably with some truth, that the sleepers were rotten anyway. The shaky state of the viaducts caused more worry and the contractors reinforced Yarde Viaduct as a precaution. Both Stowford Moor and the Torridge viaducts had been reinforced after the Great War with both timber and iron girders. G. N. Fell had been the consultant for this work.

In order to maintain a through route for the clay trains the track was often diverted around works and the quality of the diversions gave Henry Holwill more cause for complaint. Rails of insufficient weight were used and small fishplates with only two holes instead of four, for example. Andersons had been making heavy use of the line, possibly even working at night, and their skimpy repairs and temporary connections lowered the already poor standards.

This doubtless accounted for some accidents, not all of which were reported. In May 1923 four NDCC wagons were passing Summit loop at about three or four mph when one became derailed, throwing out one of Andersons' employees, who was run over and killed. At the inquest Holwill admitted that the line was not in first class condition. Another accident occurred on 18 October when two of the clay company's vans carrying their own workmen left the rails near Dunsbear and turned over. Three men were injured but fortunately not seriously.

In December 1922 it had been decided that public traffic would only be carried to Dunsbear, Clay Moor and Bury Moor, because of the use Andersons were making of the line at the time, and Watergate and Yarde sidings then closed. The traffic at the intermediate sidings was never high; Watergate in the first eight months of 1922 only handled 208 tons, with a monthly maximum of 60 tons and a minimum of but two tons. In 1918, when the local farmers were said to be particularly busy, the siding had only averaged nine tons - three wagon loads - a week.

As work on the standard-gauge progressed and the permanent way was laid a third rail was added where possible to accommodate the

A workmen's train in charge of MARY returning to the works and crossing the Rolle Road as it leaves Torrington, about 1910.
COLLECTION H. C. CASSERLEY

narrow-gauge trains. Despite great efforts there were times when Andersons had no choice but to break the link and the clay traffic had to be taken to Torrington by road, at the contractor's expense. The Southern Railway had already indicated their willingness to accept through standard-gauge trucks from Marland prior to the formal opening of the NDCJLR but the Torridge Viaduct was one of the last sections to be brought into use and it was not until the end of May 1925 that Colonel Stephens was able to work traffic through. Early in July the Southern took over the working of this traffic with their own engines and crews.

By the time the NDCJLR formally opened on 27 July 1925 the Torrington & Marland Railway had ceased to be anything more than an internal works railway. No longer did it provide a service for the local community, carrying fertiliser and coals, parcels and packages for those along its route, and there was no further use for the length beyond the pits to Bury Moor, although the track stayed in place until the 1940s. In the new role the large six-coupled locomotives were superfluous and were soon scrapped, leaving the works railway in sole command of the ex-Jersey engines. The wagons were modified with drop sides to suit new arrangements, such as the loading dock that permitted narrow-gauge wagons to be emptied direct into the standard-gauge.

The clay workers travelled out from Torrington and Yarde by the 6.25am train to Dunsbear Halt. A short walk took them to the truncated end of the three-foot gauge main line where the shanties, the workmen's carriages, would be waiting to take them to the works and the pits. This pattern persisted until British Railways stopped the passenger service in 1965, following which busses were hired to bring the men to the works to pick up the shanties. Having deposited the workers, the shanties were returned to the works, to be left standing on the old main-line ready for the following morning's run.

The clay miners had a daily allotment of clay to extract, known as a 'hag', and once they had achieved this they were free to go home. This

MARLAND waiting to leave the works, probably soon after the Great War. The young boy standing on the right is E. A. Holwill. This is probably the same occasion as the photograph on page 31.
B. D. HUGHES

In this 1913 photograph clay is being loaded from a stack, possibly it has been weathered. The Lewin-built PETER is at the head.
AUTHOR'S COLLECTION

meant that each team finished at different times, hence there was no scheduled return working of the workmen's train. One shanty was taken out at the end of the day to pick up the pitmen, who worked fixed hours, and they were able to catch the 4.46pm from Dunsbear Halt.

Having returned the morning shanties to the works, the locomotive spent the morning shunting wagons around the brickyard area. In the afternoon the loaded wagons were brought in from the pits and empties left at each shaft head for the following day's extraction. One locomotive tended to work the brickyard and two worked on the moors. There may have been an engine shed on the moors at one time. A team of three men looked after the track and the two carpenters and the blacksmith primarily worked on railway needs.

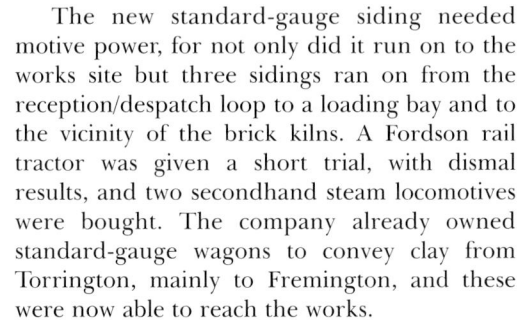

The new standard-gauge siding needed motive power, for not only did it run on to the works site but three sidings ran on from the reception/despatch loop to a loading bay and to the vicinity of the brick kilns. A Fordson rail tractor was given a short trial, with dismal results, and two secondhand steam locomotives were bought. The company already owned standard-gauge wagons to convey clay from Torrington, mainly to Fremington, and these were now able to reach the works.

As before the narrow-gauge railway around the mines was moved and re-arranged from time to time to suit new workings and the track mileage could total as much as 3½ miles (5.5 km). Precise details of developments have not survived but the area known as Grange Moor was opened up by the early part of the 1900s and it is here that all later major developments have taken place.

At the works were separate standard and narrow-gauge engine sheds, a wagon repair shop where wagons were latterly built by the company's carpenters, a sawmill for producing sleepers and pit props, and all were served by rail, of course, as were the various drying and storage sheds that had gone up higgledy-piggledy around the site. A trans-shipment siding connected the two systems, the narrow-gauge being elevated above the standard for ease of tipping clay. The weighbridge in recent years had a simple two-aspect colour light signal to control trains across its plate.

The track was always laid with flat-bottom rail, of 30 lb, 45 lb and 60 lb per yard weight.

Fell's 1879 specification required square oak sleepers but in late years at least some track was on round sleepers, making walking the line on a wet day with one's boots covered in slippery clay a treacherous business indeed. The rail came from a variety of sources, both new and second-hand, and each batch of heavier rail displaced lighter rail to be used in sidings.

Wagons of clay were worked from the pits and shaftheads in trains to the main works area where the clay was stored or taken for shredding. Return trips took wooden pit props for the mines and, when necessary, special loads of equipment. Coal was also taken out to the stationary engines that wound the mines prior to electrification.

The railways, of both gauges, served their respective purposes well and with little change as the years went by. One major change which came first to the standard-gauge in 1945 and to the narrow two years later was the introduction of diesel power. Within a few years the steam locomotives were all scrapped but the railway continued as, because of the marshy nature of the ground, no roads ran across the clay moors and the railway provided the sole means of communication.

However, in 1971 following the change of management recounted elsewhere, the railway that was once at the forefront of development was deemed to be out of date. Large open-cast pits were the new order of the day, instead of numerous small mines, and whilst the railway

A rare photograph at one of the intermediate sidings. AVONSIDE *placing wagons into Watergate siding.* JOHN ALSOP COLLECTION

Fowler diesel FORWARD *takes a train across the weigh-bridge. Note the end wagon, a Birmingham built one, has a full-length door on one side only. The engine shed is on the left.* NORTH DEVON CLAY CO.

A train of shredded clay heads to the works, hauled by FORWARD. Note the first and third wagons are Birmingham built and retain the single short door on this side.
NORTH DEVON CLAY CO.

could satisfactorily serve a static shafthead it could not do so adequately at the ever changing working face of an expanding quarry. Road vehicles had developed and could now do this, of course, and change was inevitable. Roadways were laid out to the mines and pits and on 6 November 1971 the narrow-gauge railway closed. Scrapping commenced almost immediately and little escaped the burner's torch and the bonfire. A couple of diesel locomotives and wagons have been preserved but it is the rails in particular that have continued to give service to the narrow-gauge world. Some had come to Marland from the Lynton & Barnstaple Railway, when that closed in 1935, and moved on to carry passengers again on the Llanberis Lake Railway in North Wales, and on the Seaton Tramway in East Devon. So despite not achieving its own centenary the Torrington & Marland Railway, in part at least, lives on.

A train passes between the weighbridge and the engine shed at the works. To the left of the shed is the line running up to the carpenters' shops. October 1967.
M. J. MESSENGER

On a wet day in October 1967, a Ruston waits at Grange Moor to return to the works at the end of the day. M. J. MESSENGER

TRAFFIC OVER THE TORRINGTON & MARLAND RAILWAY:

	1898	1899	1900	1908	1910	1911	1913	1921
Clay	17,179	12,472	15,112	27,000	26,847	27,279	34,000	15,580
Brick	4,182	4,698	6,225	3,300	3,994	3,498	4,000	210
Coal	1,730	1,601	1,860	1,000	1,763	1,959	2,000	550
Gravel	178	336	31					
Sundries	36	15	16					
Total NDCC traffic	23,305	19,122	23,244	31,300	32,604	32,736	40,000	16,610
Public traffic:								
Goods, manure, coal etc	2,652	2,714	2,410				2,500	1,950
Parcels & light goods	43	64	52					
Total Known traffic	26,000	31,900	25,706	31,300	32,604	31,736	42,500	18,560

Note: There are no official figures as such for traffic over the NDCC railway and the above are compiled from a number of sources whose authenticity appears reasonably acceptable. Some, such as 1908 and 1913, may be estimates while even those such as 1898 and 1899, which appear precise, coincidentally total to a round figure. At best, therefore, these figures should only be regarded as a guide.

With closure close one of the Fowler-Marshalls and a shanty wait their fate. October 1971.
ROGER HATELEY

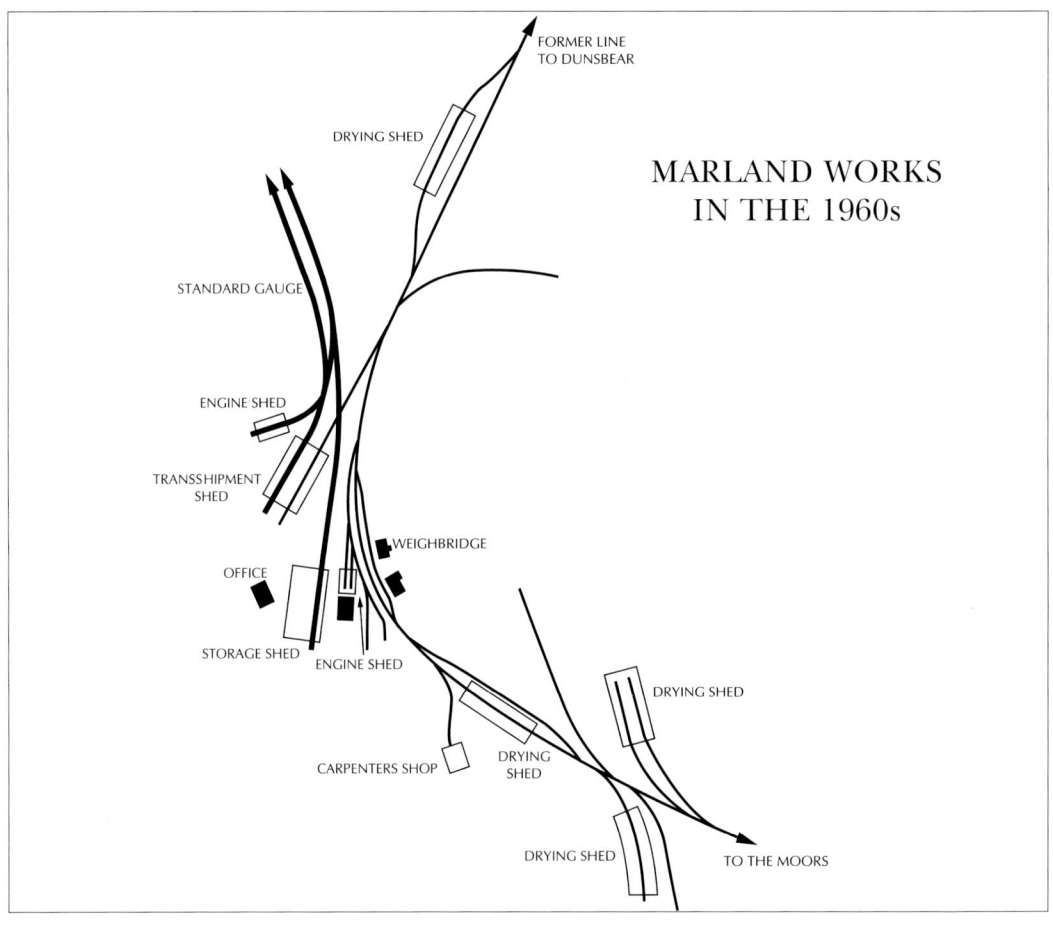

MARLAND WORKS IN THE 1960s

CHAPTER FOUR
JOHN BARRACLOUGH FELL AND THE VIADUCTS

By the latter half of the nineteenth century Britain was, in the main, well served by railways and it was becoming apparent to many that the areas that remained unserved by the railway network, mainly rural and sparsely populated, could not support the cost of a railway built to and operated to main-line standards. It was also apparent that many branch lines, often conceived as part of a grander scheme, were not paying their way and never would do.

To meet this problem, and to save many parts of the country from having to rely on the horse and cart for ever, a growing school of thought was urging the adoption of so-called 'light railways'. These would be built to a lower standard than normally accepted and thus have a lower capital cost. With a relaxation of the Board of Trade's stringent safety regulations a lower operating cost could also be achieved and the concept caught the imagination of many people.

Some favoured standard gauge, to give compatibility with the national system, while others promoted narrow gauge, with its many economies. Some protagonists were motivated, as so many in Victorian times, by the common good, introducing ideas from abroad, but others had an axe to grind in that they had technological ideas to promote. Robert Fairlie, for example, felt that his unique, and patented, articulated locomotive with its compact power could increase the viability of narrow gauge railways.

John Barraclough Fell too had a strong vested interest in promoting light and narrow gauge railways in that he made a living building them and also had patented a number of specific ideas. Fell had been born in 1815, of an old Furness family, and whilst in his twenties took a growing part in his father's timber business. The late 1840s saw the growth of the railway era and Fell became involved in local railway building. This led him on to railway construction in Italy and the mountains inspired his development of the 'centre-rail system' to enable railways to ascend steep gradients. The original railway opened in 1868 over the Mont Cenis Pass of the Alps, between France and Italy, was on this system – which was later applied in Brazil; on the Rimutaka incline in New Zealand; and is still operating, albeit in a modified form, on the Snaefell Mountain Railway in the Isle of Man.

Fell later spent a good deal of time experimenting with railways and in particular tried to develop an inexpensive quickly-laid railway, with military use especially in mind. There is a clear line of evolution in Fell's ideas, revealed in the numerous patents he took out. A short-lived and unsuccessful monorail evolved into an eight-inch gauge line and in 1872 an experimental eighteen-inch gauge line was built at Aldershot for the Royal Engineers. This line was carried on a continuous timber viaduct to dispense with earthworks, undulations in the ground surface being compensated for by varying the height of the viaduct. To add stability horizontal guide wheels were provided. The Army did not take up the idea and the journal *Engineering* asked 'whether it is worth while doing so much to gain so little'. Fell's ideas did not always receive universal acclamation and he later conceded that a wider gauge, up to three feet, was preferable and, being more stable, eliminated the need for guide wheels. By 1881 he had long put monorails and guide wheels behind him.

A conventional railway, as a modern motorway, was built on the 'cut and fill' principle whereby valleys and depressions are filled by embankments created from the material excavated from cuttings. A proportion of cuttings are planned in order to provide the fill for embankments.

Fell's idea for economy and speed of construction was to lay the track on the surface of the ground with as little excavation as possible. Where embankments would have been

John Barraclough Fell, drawn from a very poor photograph.
JANE TOWNSEND

This diagram, although by a contemporary of Fell's, illustrates the principles of his system of using viaducts in place of earthworks. It was presented at a meeting Fell attended in 1878.

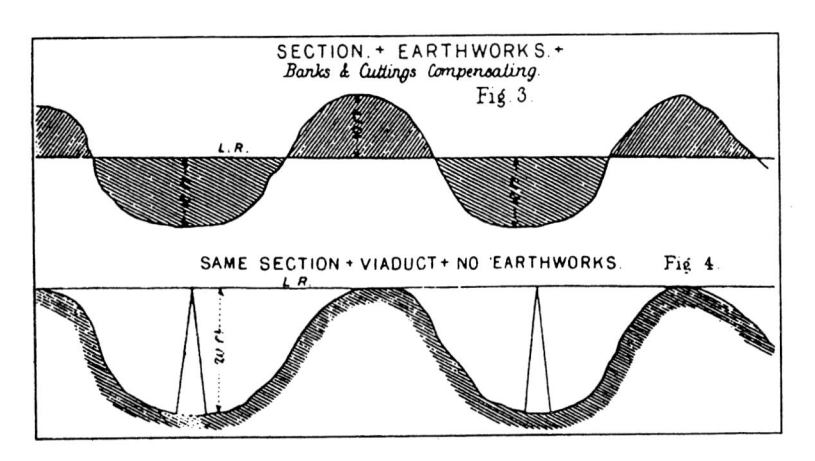

41

necessary the rails were to be carried on longitudinal girders or beams supported on iron or wooden frames. With his son, George Noble Fell, he patented the scheme in 1873 and the patent drawings show simple frames designed to be prefabricated in a workshop for speedy erection on site. Significantly, in that year Fell was rebuilding the Pentewan Railway, in Cornwall, to a 2 feet 6 inches gauge steam railway. However, he was only to be involved in a conversion of an existing railway with a satisfactory trackbed taking an easy course down the valley floor and the proposed extensions which might have used his patent system were never built. The result was, apart from the appearance of the early locomotives - whose long wheelbase indicated a need to spread their weight on, for example, flimsy viaducts - little obvious signs of Fell's theories.

The Torrington & Marland Railway was to be different for this was a new railway through varied country, ranging from steep narrow valleys to open moors. It must have been with this in mind that another patent, in J. B. Fell's sole name, was taken out in 1879 for this showed an improved design of support, or viaduct, much more suitable for the rough country south of Torrington than the 1873 patent, and this improved design was as depicted in the contract drawings for the railway.

The piers consisted of two or more timber uprights braced together by diagonal crossties to form a lattice and resting on a frame or on sleepers firmly embedded in the ground. Timber girders of lattice construction spanned the gap between the piers and carried the rails. The following year another patent improved the design by adding strengthening struts, in particular inclined stays which could be extensions of the girder lattices, and these were to give greater strength and stability. Photographs show that the T&MR viaducts were constructed to these later plans.

The use of wood for major engineering structures was common in this period. Brunel was one of the most well known engineers to do so but lesser engineers did also; Arthur Cadlick Pain, for example, who built the Culm Valley Light Railway and other minor lines in the west country. It was economical and readily available in suitable strengths from home and overseas.

The viaducts were quite distinctive structures, if not unique, and bore little resemblance to the better known timber viaducts of Brunel. The West Country had many successful examples of the latter - some were to last nearly seventy years - and one may wonder why Fell should develop a different design. However, he was an innovator and an inventor and to be different seems to have been part of his nature. The supports of Brunel's viaducts radiate from their bases like a fan, supporting the track with diagonal cross-bracing. Other Victorian engineers used similar radiating supports. While Fell used some cross-bracing on larger spans most supports were simple verticals, at right-angles to the track, and to the lay person they would seem much weaker laterally. But, despite minimal maintenance for much of their life, some of the Marland viaducts did last for over forty years.

Fell saw in the Marland line the opportunity to build a light railway illustrating his principles and to use it as a demonstration. The order for the first locomotive stated, unusually, that it was 'to pass Government inspection'. As a private railway the T&MR would not be inspected by any Government department, except by request. There was some military interest in the line, and overseas interest, but whether it bore any fruit for Fell is doubtful. Certainly his methods worked as regards time and cost. The six-mile line was completed, almost, in the six months laid down for its construction and, although the cost was 50% more than the tender the final cost of £2,400 per mile was still very economical. One unusual effect of Fell's theories was to give the three locomotives ordered for working the main line very long wheel-bases - nine feet - in order to spread their weight.

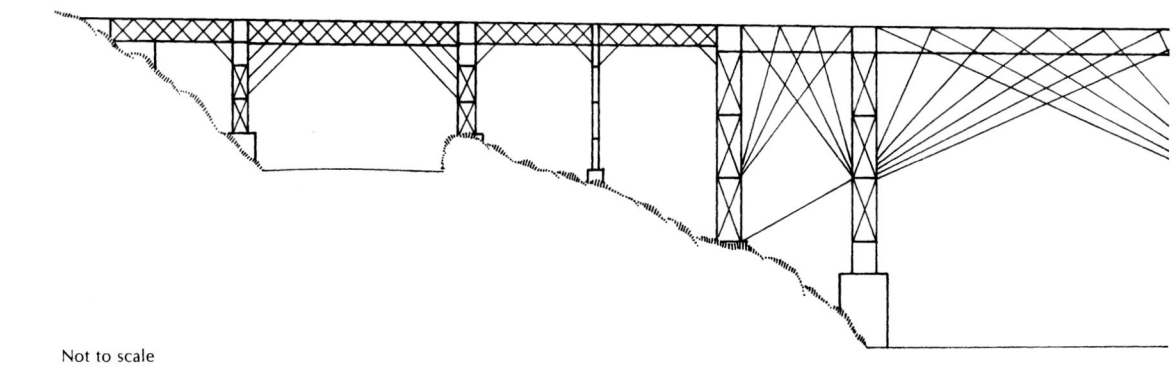

Whilst not a scale drawing this is correctly in proportion, including the falling gradient across the viaduct.

Not to scale

Yarde Viaduct in process of being filled in by Andersons as part of the NDCJLR contract. Doing the job is their GYP and train of side-tipping wagons. The additional piers probably erected by the contractors are prominent.
E. A. HOLWILL

Exactly how many 'viaducts' the line had is not clear. A contemporary newspaper report states ten but this evidently included quite small bridges over streams which utilised Fell's timber girders, some of which were so insignificant as to escape the notice of the Ordnance Survey mappers. Such a bridge would have been that just north of Watergate crossing the river. In order to be a 'viaduct' rather than a mere 'bridge' a structure should have two or more arches and there were the large Torridge Viaduct and at least five, and perhaps more, lower shorter ones.

Photographs of the latter type show shallow structures perhaps eighteen feet high with piers of single vertical uprights and track supported on timber lattice girders. The Ordnance Survey large-scale maps and a few photographs are almost the only positive information we have regarding these viaducts and the differences recorded between the OS surveys of 1884-85 and 1906 show that all viaducts were shortened and some replaced. The table summarises these changes.

Viaduct	Span 1884-85	Span 1906
Torridge	316 yards (287m)	316 yards (287m)
Barley Hayes	45 yards (41m)	24 feet (7m)
Langtree Wick	50 yards (46m)	Deviation built 1902
Stowford Moor	280 yards (265m)	105 yards (96m)
Yarde	275 yards (251m)	230 yards (210m)
Speccott	82 yards (75m)	Embankment

Several viaducts had their piers reinforced with brick and a photograph of Yarde taken in the 1920s shows at least five substantial brick piers had been built as reinforcement, although this was possibly done by Andersons. Langtree Wick, half a mile south-east of Barley Hayes, crossed a narrow but steep side-valley on nine or ten piers up to about twenty feet high. It was replaced by a deviation of some 280 yards (256m) a few yards to the west during 1902. The gang that did the job was to continue and fill in

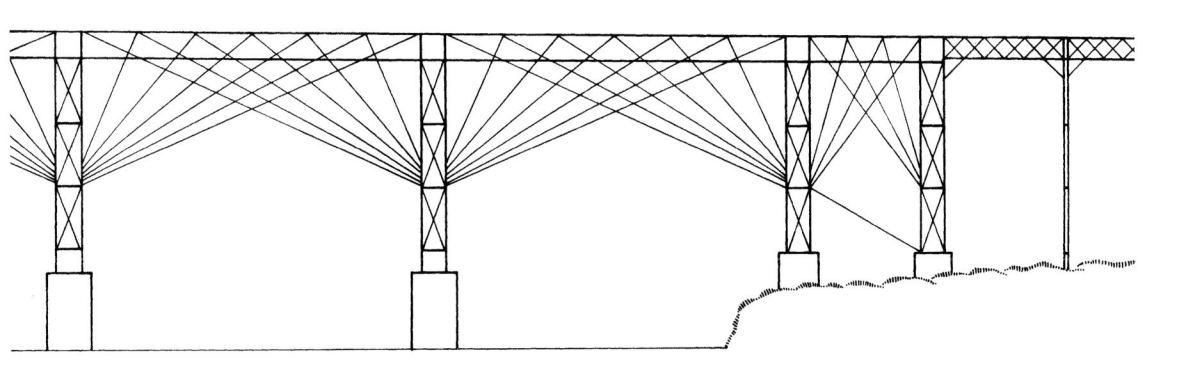

The main spans of the Torridge Viaduct soon after construction. The cutwaters appear to be timber and the short lengths of handrail on the side-spans were soon removed. These may be the remains of full length handrails.
COLLECTION B. D. HUGHES

Yarde Viaduct if they had no other work but we know they did not get very far. Speccott Viaduct was very low, perhaps no more than twelve feet, and had been replaced by an embankment by 1906. In 1920 Henry Holwill said they had three viaducts which must have been Torridge, Stowford and Yarde.

The viaduct at Barley Hayes, reduced by 1906 to a single span of 24 feet (7m), was giving trouble in 1903 and amongst the brickwork of the later NDCJLR arch bridge the stone abutments of the T&MR bridge can be seen.

South of Dunsbear, on the section unrebuilt by the NDCJLR, the 1885 Ordnance Survey shows a viaduct but this is now just a small brick arch and presumably it was rebuilt. Further south where the line crossed the River Mere there could have been another viaduct but evidence is lacking.

Fell's *piéce-de-résistance*, of course, was the spectacular viaduct across the River Torridge, just outside Torrington station. Overall it was more than 300 yards long but the main section consisted of five spans crossing the river itself; three of 45 feet (14m) each flanked by shorter spans of about 18 feet (5.4m) each. The six square section timber piers were extensively cross-braced and from these sprang the fan-like diagonals which provided support for the track. The piers were supported on brick bases and the two in the river sported brick cutwaters. The rails were 38 feet (12m) above the river and the piers piled 12 feet (3.65m) into the bed.

To the north of the river spans, connecting

with the solid ground at the cutting approach to the short tunnel under the main road, were four more spans, the longest of which crossed the Rolle Road. This was later (about 1913) replaced by an iron girder span and at least one of the piers by brick.

On the south side it took forty-two spans to cross the gently sloping river meadows to the embankment that then carried the line into the wooded Pencleave Valley. Each span was of 15 feet (4.57m) and supported on timber piers of the simplest type - similar to Yarde - decreasing in height southwards. The piers had no solid foundation but were merely buried 18 inches to two feet in the ground.

No plans of the bridge survive for, as mentioned above, the contract drawings do not depict exactly what was built. However, with the aid of photographs and a few key measurements from contemporary sources the drawings do form a valuable guide to the structure. Despite the modifications to the plans, apparent from the second patent, certain basic features would not alter. The timber used in the main vertical supports was eight inches by four inches section and the remainder four inches by three. The small lattice girder spans were 15 feet (4.57m) long and the depth of the girder two feet (60cm) or thirty inches (76cm); photographs show the latter in use.

Fell himself is quoted as stating the length of the Torridge Viaduct to be 266 yards but the 25-inch Ordnance Survey map indicates a length of approximately 316 yards and the writer, after detailed examination of more than a dozen photographs, considers this figure correct. The southern approach (42 spans of 15 feet) appears to be 210 yards, the river section 57 yards, and the Rolle Road bridge section 25 yards, making 292 yards. A further 24 yards for the widths of the fifty piers is not inappropriate and makes a total of 316 yards (287m) in all. It seems strange that Fell should err in the length, and a journalistic error is more likely.

The type of timber used for all viaducts was Baltic red pine. It was not until the early twentieth century, after twenty or thirty years' use, that repairs to the viaducts begin to appear in the minute books as an urgent topic. Later

Langtree Wick viaduct with MARY heading south. A number of factors suggest this was taken in the very early days of the railway. MARY is in original condition, with an open cab, and the single wagon may contain an inspection party. The snow reinforces this although bad winters were quite common then. Furthermore the source of the picture is Fell family papers.
F. KEITH PEARSON

This very shallow viaduct is almost certainly Speccott, which was replaced by an embankment by 1906. MARY now has a cab but no back and is facing Torrington. It also appears to have some form of spark arrester on the chimney.
F. KEITH PEARSON

NORTH DEVON CLAY

The new piers of the NDCJLR viaduct can be seen in front of the T&MR viaduct, linked by temporary contractor's tracks. Comparison with the photographs on pages 35 and 44 reveals the changes made to the old viaduct; the replacement of the Rolle Road spans with steel girders and the reinforcement of the timber uprights with brickwork. Note the vertical boiler on the left providing a power source. E. A. HOLWILL

photographs show increased bracing and supports and the masonry supporting several of the piers of the Torridge Viaduct was extended upwards to embrace the timber.

The construction of the NDCJLR saw the replacement of the remaining viaducts; the Torridge Viaduct by a modern girder structure alongside and the others by embankments. The bases of some of the old piers in the river survived for a good number of years. Despite their unconventional design they served the line for more than forty years, playing a major part in providing the economical line of communication that was so essential to the North Devon Clay Company, and perhaps it is on this that J. B. Fell and his timber viaducts should be judged.

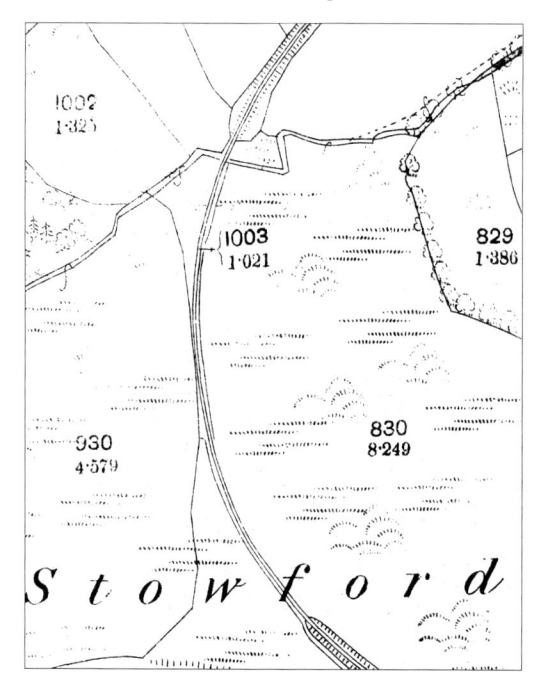

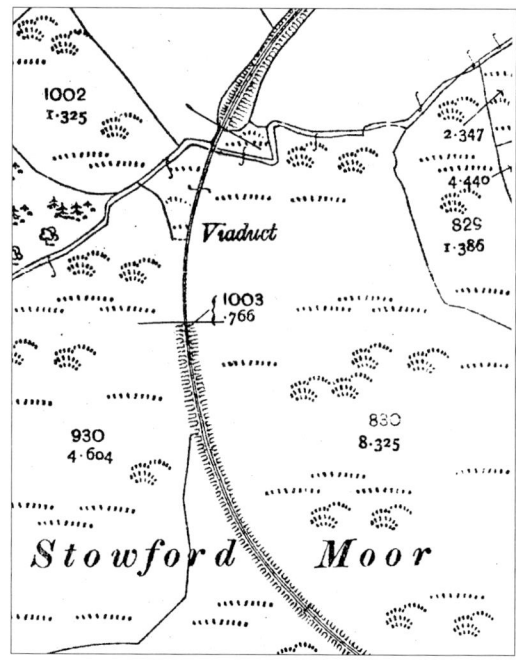

These extracts from two editions, 1887 and 1906, of the 25-inch Ordnance Survey show how Stowford Moor viaduct was reduced in length.

46

CHAPTER FIVE
LOCOMOTIVES AND ROLLING STOCK OF MARLAND

The motive power of the Torrington & Marland Railway and of the North Devon Clay Co. Ltd. was almost as varied as it could possibly be. It can be categorised in so many ways - narrow-gauge and standard, main-line and works, steam and diesel - that the object of categorising is defeated. Only in later years was there any attempt at standardisation, and prior to that practically every locomotive came from a different manufacturer.

There were certain features in common, however, and this was most apparent on those locomotives used for the run between the works and Torrington, the main-line engines. There were eventually three of these, *Mary*, *Marland* and *Avonside*, and all were six-coupled tanks featuring a very long wheelbase, nine feet. This was dictated by Fell's timber viaducts - the purpose being to spread the weight as much as possible. A result of this was flangeless centre driving wheels to enable the engines to negotiate curves. Another feature dictated by the steep gradients, often through wooded country, was the sandboxes; *Avonside* was designed with four, and the others seem to have been as well provided. Open-back cabs were fitted when the locomotives were new but closed backs were added, possibly at the works, to give the crews protection from the weather. All three main-line engines were scrapped soon after the opening of the NDCJLR in 1925.

Fell's original intention was that coupling should have been by combined centre buffer-couplings of the chopper variety. The makers' drawings of the wagons and *Avonside* show this and photographs of the three main-line engines show that they were at least fitted with buffers of this type, although no choppers were fitted when the photographs were taken. It may be that the track around the works and clay mines was too irregular for this type of semi-automatic coupling and made the use of side-chains essential. The centre buffer was retained and coupling achieved by a pair of side-chains.

The works locomotives were all four-wheeled and, in the main, quite small and light. The powerful Fletcher Jennings engines were the exception and their weight problem was solved in a unique way. The works locomotives were steam powered until the late 1940s when diesels were introduced and the latter were disposed of when the narrow-gauge rail system was dismantled in 1970.

For a long period heavy engineering work that was beyond the capacity of the works' facilities was handled by Hodges Bros. in Exeter. One intriguing minute of 1894 states that 'Mr Hodges would repair and compound the engines at a cost of about £20 and as the alteration would effect a saving in fuel (estimated at one-third) it was resolved that it be carried out as early as possible.' Compounding railway engines would be difficult and one must assume this refers to the stationary engines around the works. Whether it happened is not known. For major boiler work Henry Holwill tended to shop around for the cheapest quote, rather than go to the relevant manufacturer who, with the original drawings, would have found the job easier. Much work was done by Abbott & Co, the Newark Boiler Works.

One idiosyncrasy at Marland which was common to all the narrow-gauge steam locomotives was the bracket on each smokebox on which sat the tallow kettle. The thus warmed tallow would be readily available to lubricate the locomotive and its train, and the kettle can be seen in many photographs.

One of the main sources of information for this chapter, the article in *The Locomotive* in 1913, states that the locomotives were numbered in the same series as the stationary engines used at the works and mines and it can be implied from the minute books that in fact the numbers referred to the boilers. This is borne out by a boiler insurance policy of 1891 which has much useful information. There are implications that the numbers changed from time to time, when reboilering took place. Photographic evidence confirms that no numbers were carried.

Similarly names were allocated to many of the engines, steam and diesel, but only some of the latter appear to have carried them. Of the names themselves, the origins of some, such as *Marland*, *Mersey* or *Jersey* are self-explanatory, but *Peter* is not known. One can only speculate that *Mary* might have been named after G. N. Fell's wife, who died just before its delivery. Alternatively, it could have been named after one of the sisters of W. A. B. Wren, although the other sister was not honoured. The livery of the steam locomotives was unlined dark green and

47

Black, Hawthorn Works No. – 576 0-6-0T Built 1880

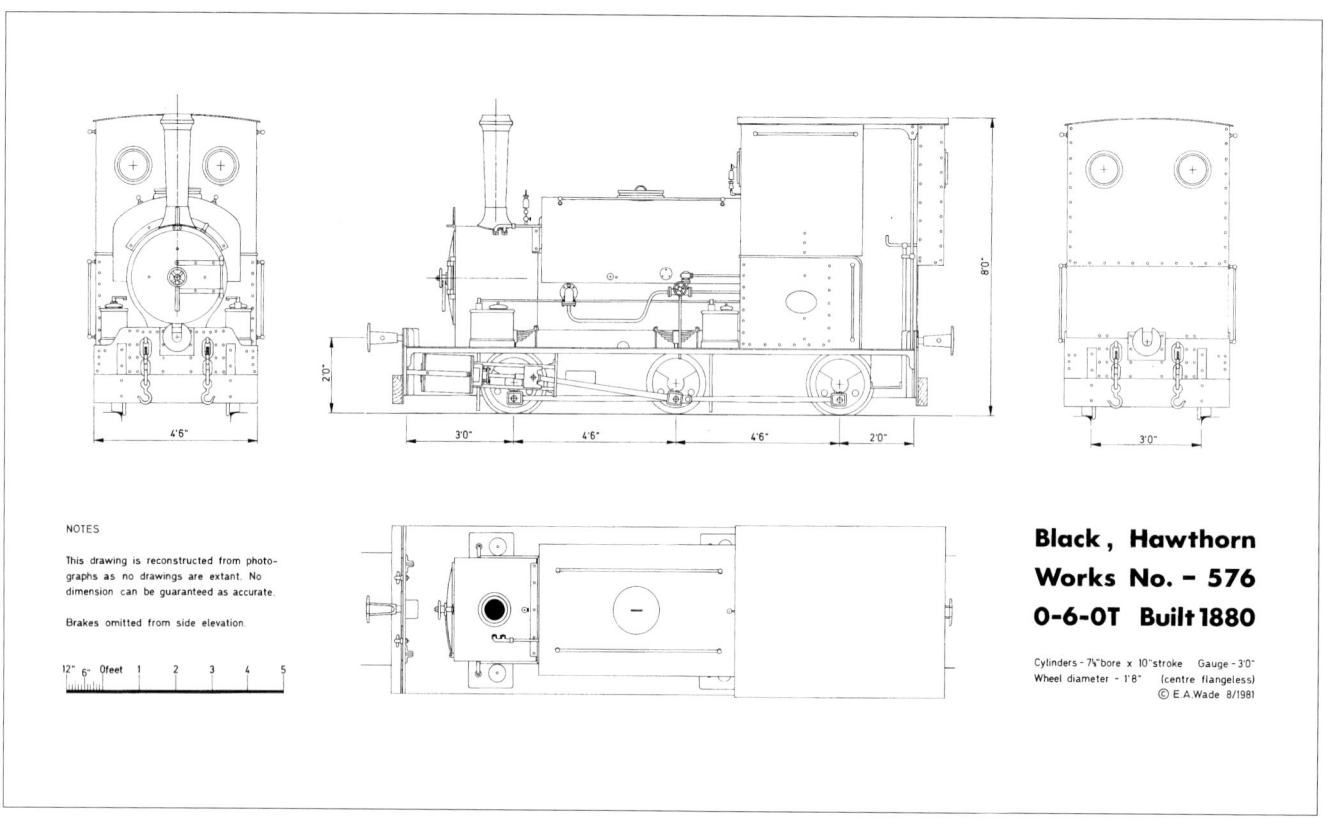

Cylinders - 7¼"bore x 10"stroke   Gauge - 3'0"
Wheel diameter - 1'8"   (centre flangeless)
© E.A.Wade 8/1981

NOTES
This drawing is reconstructed from photographs as no drawings are extant. No dimension can be guaranteed as accurate.

Brakes omitted from side elevation.

MARY outside the engine shed with additions to the cab. Behind can be glimpsed a Jersey engine dating it after 1910. LOCOMOTIVE CLUB OF GREAT BRITAIN, KEN NUNN COLLECTION.

the diesels were painted in the standard green liveries of the manufacturers.

The locomotives' individual histories, as known, are given below in chronological order of acquisition, first narrow-gauge and then standard. There are no official records to draw from but it is hoped that this account is as complete as research has permitted. Formal details of all the locomotives are given in an appendix.

In view of the doubtful disposal of some of the locomotives it may be as well to dismiss a red herring which briefly sidetracked the writer. In his acutely observed story *Tarka the Otter* Henry Williamson relates how an old dog-otter called Marland Jimmy used to hide in the funnel of 'a rusted, weedgrown engine that had lain for years half-buried in the clayey ooze' of the White Clay Pits. Alas the author had not stumbled across one of the North Devon Clay Co.'s missing locomotives, for Williamson translated this scene from a limestone quarry elsewhere.

NARROW-GAUGE LOCOMOTIVES

Mary

J. B. Fell ordered the T&MR's first locomotive, a six-coupled saddle-tank, from Black Hawthorn & Co. Ltd, of Gateshead, in June 1880 in the name of the 'Marland & Torrington Railway Co'. It was required 'to be delivered in three months without fail, to be a first class job, well fitted and finished, to pass Government inspection'. Fell's bill of quantities of 1879 budgeted £850 for the purchase but the payment on delivery in December 1880 was only £750. *Mary* arrived in time to help with the final construction work and was the sole main-line motive power for three years.

The boiler insurance policy of 1891, where Mary is strangely numbered 2, gives the date of make as 1891 but as the policy is for the boiler this implies that *Mary* was reboilered that year. The safety valve is set at 140 lbs, higher than any

NOTES

This drawing is reconstructed from photographs as no drawings are extant. No dimension can be guaranteed as accurate.

Safety chains omitted from side elevation.

**W.G. Bagnall, Ltd.
Works No. – 566
0-6-0T   Built 1883**

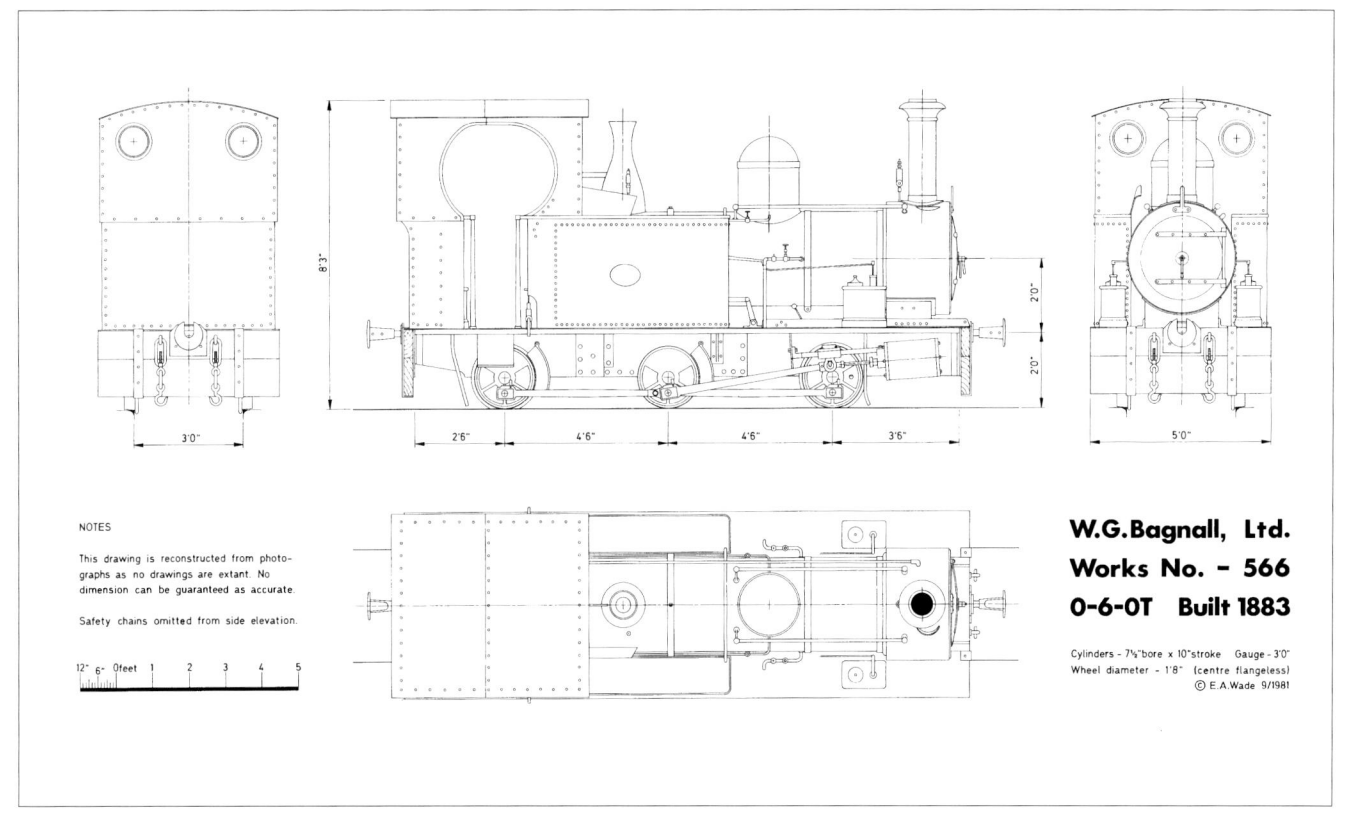

Cylinders - 7½"bore x 10"stroke   Gauge - 3'0"
Wheel diameter - 1'8" (centre flangeless)
© E.A.Wade 9/1981

other boiler suggesting it might be new. The value was £1,000. Another new boiler was fitted in 1907.

The only reference in the minutes to this locomotive was in late 1923 when the boiler was sent away for a new copper firebox. This seems strange as the demise of the railway must by then have been very apparent but Andersons were hiring the engine and may, indirectly or directly, have paid for this. With the opening of the NCDJLR Mary was superfluous and soon scrapped.

Tudor

In March 1883 a small locomotive was hired from Bagnall's. *Tudor* had been built in 1879 but exactly who it was delivered to is not known for certain, nor is it known how long it stayed at Marland, except that by January 1888 it was on a reservoir contract elsewhere. With its small cylinders and 18-inch driving wheels it was too tiny for the main-line and was no doubt for use around the works and clay pits. The hire agreement was a lease with option to purchase within 18 months. The premium was £70 and the quarterly rent £55 but there is no evidence that the locomotive was purchased. It is quite likely that when *Marland* arrived in December 1883 the two large engines were adequate to deal with all traffic.

Marland

The second main-line engine came from W. G. Bagnall Ltd, of Stafford, in December 1883, having been ordered in August by the North Devon Clay Co. It cost £565 and had a copper fire-box and brass tubes. The wheelbase was nine feet and despite being a side-tank the layout was very similar to *Mary*. A distinctive feature was the stylish safety valve cover. In 1891 *Marland* was valued at £900.

MARLAND in original condition standing on one of the timber viaducts illustrating the advantage of the long wheelbase. Compare with the later view opposite.
E. A. HOLWILL

49

MARLAND waiting to leave the works, about 1913. The extended smokebox, improved cab and other alterations are quite clear, as is the tallow kettle at the base of the chimney.
LOCOMOTIVE PUBLISHING CO.

Like *Mary* little is known of how *Marland* fared during its working life but photographs show that the cab was enclosed and the smokebox was rebuilt at some time after 1899. In 1904 *Marland* still had its original boiler but how much longer it lasted is not known. A new firebox was fitted during the Great War but due to wartime restrictions on materials a steel one was fitted instead of copper, and the locomotive performed badly as a result. The boiler was sent away for repairs in 1918 and the locomotive's prolonged absence from service put a great strain on the other two main line engines. The cost of a new boiler was sought from Bagnalls in 1920 but a new firebox was fitted instead. With the other main-line locomotives *Marland* was scrapped in 1925.

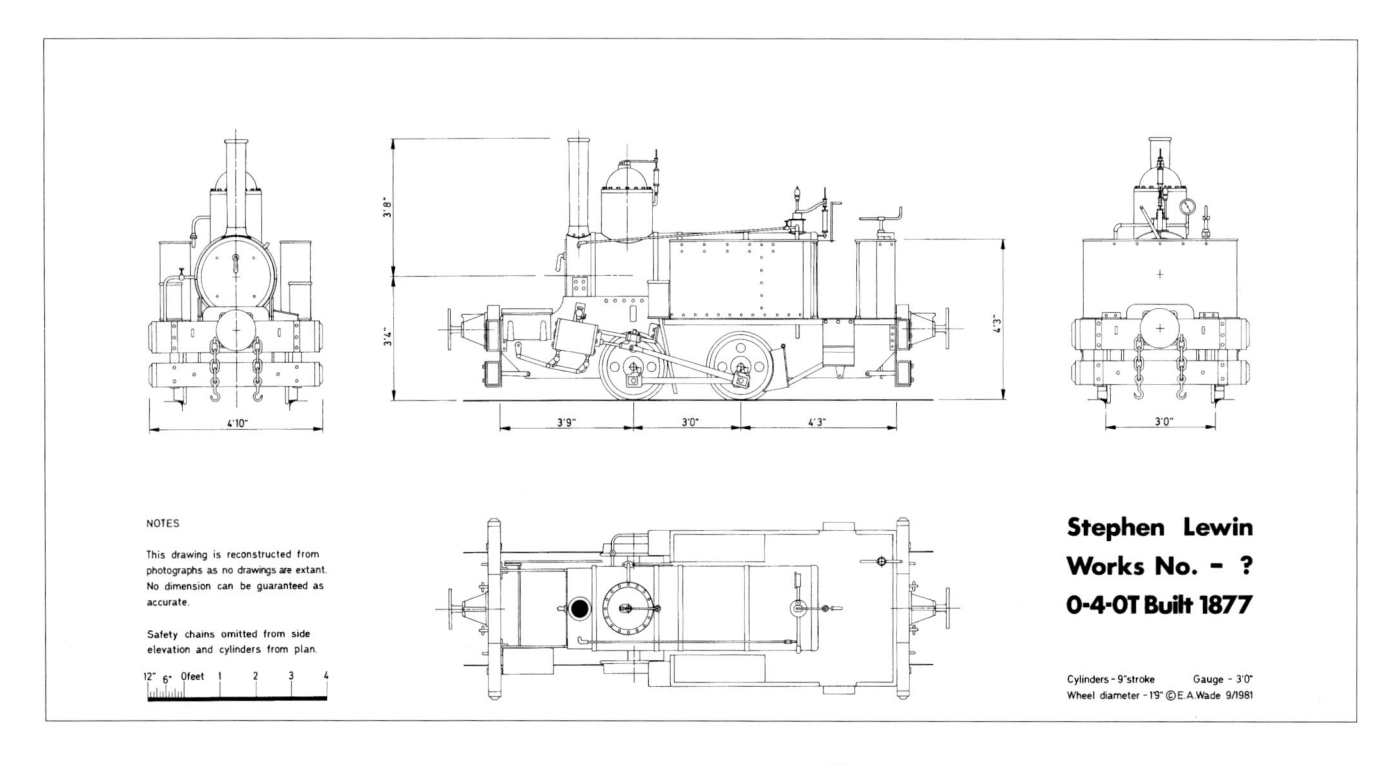

Stephen Lewin
Works No. – ?
0-4-0T Built 1877

Cylinders - 9"stroke   Gauge - 3'0"
Wheel diameter - 19" © E.A.Wade 9/1981

NOTES
This drawing is reconstructed from photographs as no drawings are extant. No dimension can be guaranteed as accurate.

Safety chains omitted from side elevation and cylinders from plan.

50

Peter

Very little is known about this little locomotive. It was one of the few products of that obscure Dorset engineer, Stephen Lewin of Poole, but when it reached Marland is unknown. Lewin's first locomotives were built in 1874 and a similar locomotive was advertised for sale by a Kent agent in 1878 but *Peter* did not arrive at Marland until at least 1884. With its short wheelbase of three feet it was ideally suited for use around the works and pits. The boiler policy of 1891 confirms that *Peter* was by then at the works and had been built in 1877. It had a launch type boiler and was valued at £450.

It was probably *Peter* that suffered the appalling accident in 1900. Although the main line locomotives were often referred to in company records by their names, or nicknames, *Peter* was usually mentioned as 'No 3' or the 'small clay loco'. A new boiler seems to have been fitted in 1905 and in September 1920, when £356 was quoted to overhaul the locomotive, it was decided the expenditure was not justified. Presumably it did not last much longer and had certainly gone by 1925, replaced by one of the Jersey locomotives, although Henry Holwill did consider 'an oil loco' to do its work. (Dimensions have been deduced from photographs or taken from those known of the Kent locomotive which may well have been Peter).

Coffeepot

Even less is known of this engine; the few sources of information include two sentences in *The Locomotive* and the 1891 boiler policy. The former stated it to have been purchased 'some years ago' at South Shields and was scrapped in about 1908. The fact that it had inclined outside cylinders suggests it was built by Head Wrightson & Co. Ltd, of Stockton-on-Tees, for this is the hallmark of such locomotives built by them in the 1870s. However, the 1891 policy gives the maker as Taylor & Bodley, of Exeter,

PETER with a family of admirers, beside one of the clay pits. This was taken quite late in its life as the wagon is locally built. LOCOMOTIVE & GENERAL RAILWAY PHOTOGRAPHS

PETER at Marland works. LOCOMOTIVE CLUB OF GREAT BRITAIN, KEN NUNN COLLECTION.

This enlargement from a poorly reproduced photograph, of about 1900, shows the vertical boiler locomotive at the head of a train of locally built wagons at the pits.
BALL CLAY HERITAGE SOCIETY

and the date 1884. Taylor & Bodley are not known as locomotive manufacturers but did manufacture boilers. They may well have provided a new boiler on its acquisition by the North Devon Clay Co. 1884 is a likely date for this. Later insurance papers suggest it was reboilered sometime and scrapped by January 1904. It was one of the two clay works locomotives mentioned in the 1893 report.

Avonside
At the end of the nineteenth century an additional engine for main-line work was urgently needed but it was not until 1900 that a decision was made to buy one, on hire purchase. Specifications were sought from Bagnall and Kerr Stuart but the order went to the Avonside Engine Co. Ltd. in Bristol in November for delivery by the following April. The locomotive was named after its manufacturer, although it

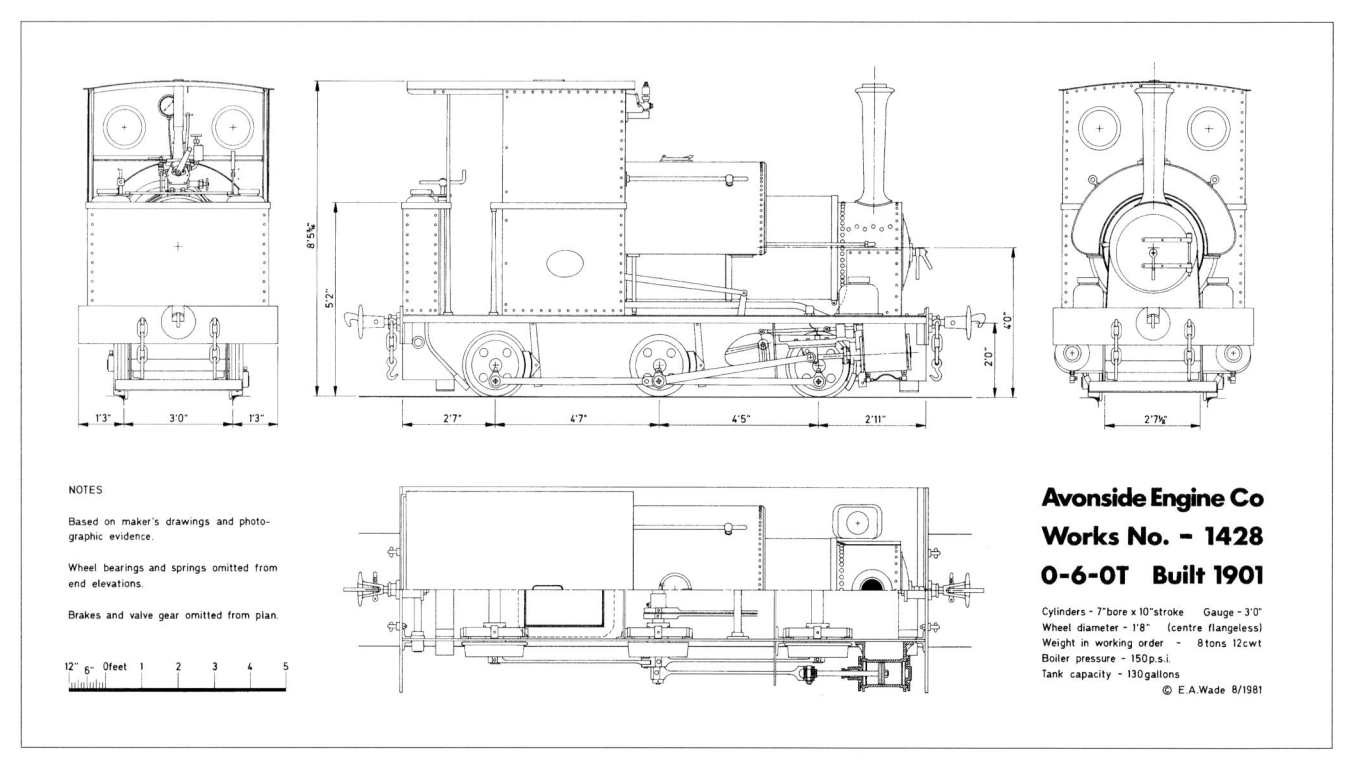

Avonside Engine Co
Works No. – 1428
0-6-0T Built 1901

Cylinders - 7"bore x 10"stroke   Gauge - 3'0"
Wheel diameter - 1'8" (centre flangeless)
Weight in working order - 8 tons 12cwt
Boiler pressure - 150 p.s.i.
Tank capacity - 130 gallons

© E.A.Wade 8/1981

NOTES
Based on maker's drawings and photographic evidence.
Wheel bearings and springs omitted from end elevations.
Brakes and valve gear omitted from plan.

The manufacturer's photograph of AVONSIDE. It is interesting to note that both chopper couplings and side-chains are fitted although by this date the chopper couplings had been discarded on the railway. The cab was enclosed later.
B. D. STOYEL

may have been more in the nature of a nickname, and followed the same style as *Mary* and *Marland*. Photographs of *Avonside* are scarce although the maker's drawings exist. There were strong similarities to *Mary* but *Avonside*'s saddle-tank was shorter and rounder in section. *Avonside* suffered during the Great War and was evidently in bad condition by 1920. Henry Holwill was afraid he might have to stop the engine before *Marland* could be returned from its overhaul. Quotes were obtained from Avonside to fit a new firebox but the locomotive could not be spared for the three months that the job would take.

Jersey I, Jersey II and Merton

The only semblance of uniformity in the Marland steam fleet came from these three 0-4-0 saddle-tanks purchased second-hand from Jersey in August 1908. They had been built in

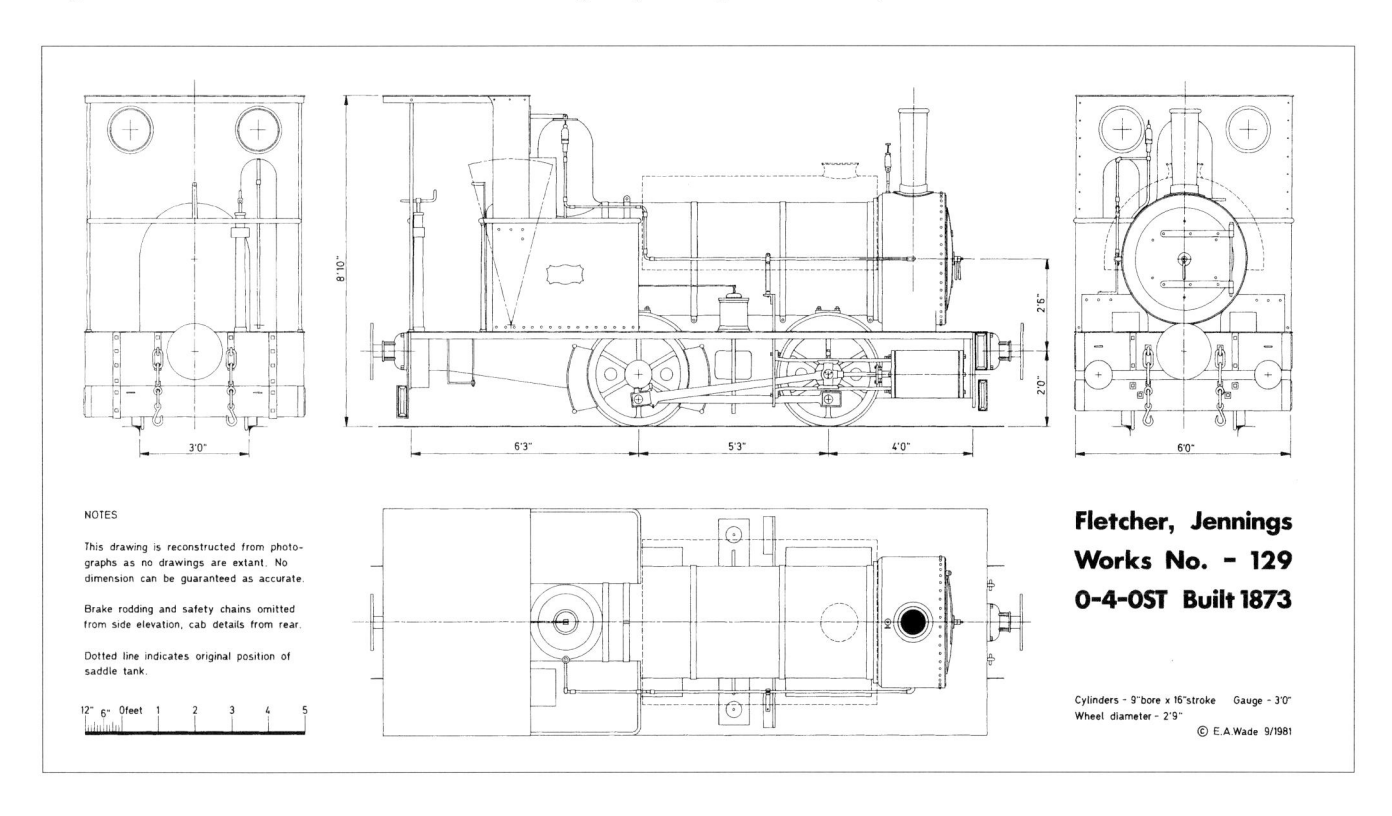

Fletcher, Jennings
Works No. - 129
0-4-0ST Built 1873

Cylinders - 9"bore x 16"stroke   Gauge - 3'0"
Wheel diameter - 2'9"

© E.A.Wade 9/1981

NOTES
This drawing is reconstructed from photographs as no drawings are extant. No dimension can be guaranteed as accurate.

Brake rodding and safety chains omitted from side elevation, cab details from rear.

Dotted line indicates original position of saddle tank.

53

The first of the Fletcher Jennings locomotives to be rebuilt for use at Marland was named JERSEY I. Seen here at Marland works with the saddle tank now sitting on a wagon frame as a tender, the photographs were taken soon after the conversion in 1910.
LOCOMOTIVE PUBLISHING CO.

A Jersey engine in rather more work-a-day condition. As these locomotives were intended to work in the clay works its presence apparently taking a train out on the main line could indicate the time is the period immediately after the Great War when motive power was difficult. With this tender this could be JERSEY I *but identification is difficult.* LOCOMOTIVE CLUB OF GREAT BRITAIN, KEN NUNN COLLECTION.

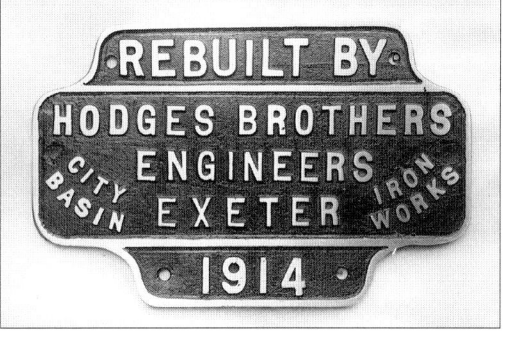

The second conversion, MERTON, *carried this plate.*
G. ALLIEZ, VIA B. D. STOYEL

The second and third Jersey engines had tenders that appeared to have come from old locomotive boilers, from either railway locomotives or the many stationary engines that were used about the works. These are two different locomotives - JERSEY II *and* MERTON *- but which is which is not known.* NORTH DEVON CLAY CO / R. W. KIDNER

the 1870s by Fletcher, Jennings & Co., at Whitehaven, and had been used on the breakwater work at St Helier. Having been idle for some years they were not in very good condition but the best of the three was rebuilt in 1910 at the works using parts of the other two locomotives. It was intended for use around the works and pits but was found too heavy for the light track so the ingenious solution was reached of mounting the saddle-tank on a wagon underframe behind the locomotive. In this guise the engine, *Jersey I*, was successful and in 1914 and 1915 the other two were rebuilt similarly as *Merton* and *Jersey II*. The first was done at the works but the second was rebuilt by Hodges Bros, at Exeter. No doubt the third locomotive was the worst and needed more doing to it. *Jersey I* had a new mild steel firebox fitted by Hodges in 1918.

At least one of these two, if not both, had what appears to be an old boiler barrel for a water tank, instead of a saddle tank. Although very similar there were minor differences in detail between the three. They were large powerful engines but despite suggestions elsewhere that they were lightened because of the viaducts this is not entirely so, for they did not work through to Torrington, on a regular basis anyway. After 1925 they provided the entire motive power requirements on the truncated works system until dieselisation. A visitor in 1942 found one of the locomotives working whilst *Merton* was in the shed, out of steam. A driver confirmed that a third engine

Diesel line-up at Marland. From left to right: narrow gauge ADVANCE *and* FORWARD, *standard gauge* PROGRESS, *narrow gauge* EFFICIENCY *and standard gauge* PETER. NORTH DEVON CLAY CO. LTD.

had formerly been kept for shunting at the pits, suggesting it had been scrapped, but the visitor found the remains of what might possibly have been it in a shed nearby. Industrial Railway Society records indicate that two were scrapped in 1949 and the last in 1952.

Forward

Following the success of the standard-gauge diesels, one was ordered new from John Fowler & Co (Leeds) Ltd for the narrow-gauge and arrived in August 1947. It was of 40hp and of Fowler's 'Resilient' type, and evidently gave little trouble for it was this type that was asked for when Fowlers were offered a repeat order in 1959. *Forward* tended to be used around the brick yard and was scrapped in November 1970.

Advance *and* Efficiency

The next two narrow-gauge diesels to arrive at Marland give the lie to the oft-quoted statement that diesels are but characterless boxes on wheels, although some of the character could probably have been done without in this case. *Advance*, delivered in December 1949, and *Efficiency*, delivered eighteen months later, were a result of Fowler's links with Marshall, Sons & Co. Ltd, of Gainsborough. The latter had developed a successful agricultural tractor, named the 'Field-Marshall' and Fowlers had

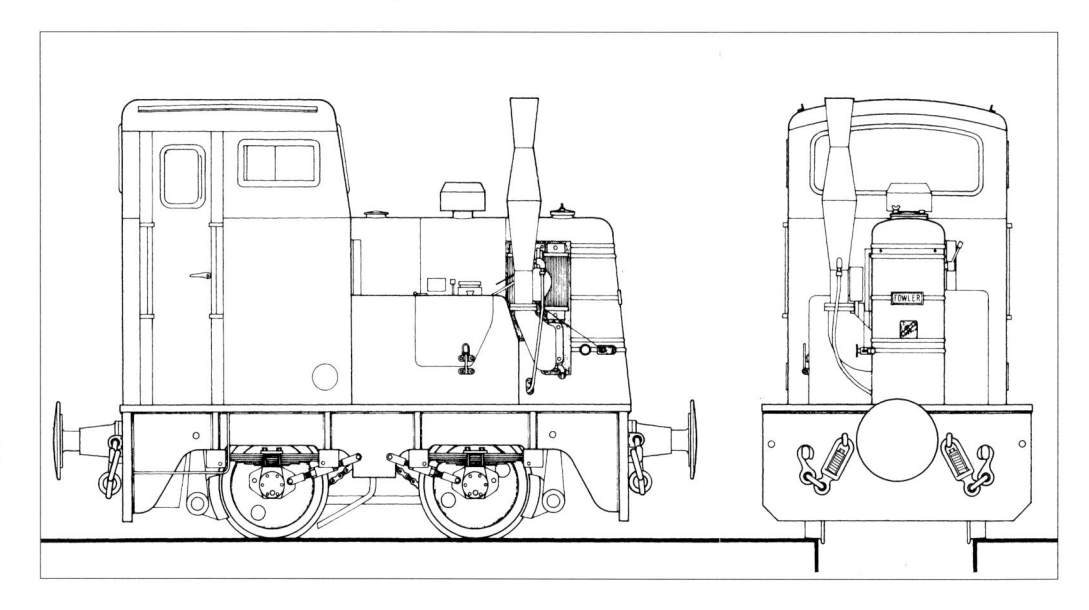

A Marshall-engined diesel locomotive by John Fowler & Co. Ltd. This drawing is derived from one of the type elsewhere in England and adapted from photographic evidence to represent one of those at Marland. R. E. WEST

The Fowler Marshall locomotives sat abandoned behind the works for a good number of years. May 1968.
M. J. MESSENGER

endeavoured to utilise its single-cylinder two-stroke engine in a locomotive design. They were not common in this country although a lot more went abroad.

The locomotives weighed 7¼ tons and the rugged engine developed 40hp but the many advantages of the simple design were not so apparent in practice. The vibration of the single cylinder may well have accounted for many of the problems. Initially, at least, *Efficiency* was the worst of the two and trouble was experienced with poor starting (a cartridge being used when cold), gear selection and the engine working loose from its mountings. Watching the vibrations of a preserved Field-Marshall tractor at a vintage rally gives a good idea of the problems the locomotives suffered from. They were not popular and were replaced by the Ruston & Hornsby diesels, although they survived in dismantled form until the 1970s. *Advance* was scrapped with *Forward* but *Efficiency* was preserved elsewhere in Devon.

RUSTON & HORNSBY DIESELS

When further diesel locomotives were sought in 1959 Fowlers no longer manufactured locomotives as small as 40hp and Ruston & Hornsby Ltd, Lincoln, were turned to. In due course four of their products were bought for the narrow-gauge, three of type 48DL. The first was bought new in 1959 and a second, which took over the name *Efficiency* from the Fowler, in 1961. They were of 48hp and driven mechanically by roller chains. A third, bought second-hand in 1965 for spares, had been built in 1959 for underground use. The fourth locomotive, bought new in 1965, was of type LFT and also of 48hp but the chain drive was *via* a Dowty Hydrostatic transmission. At closure of the system the oldest Ruston went to the Seaton & District Electric Tramway in East Devon, where it was regauged to two feet nine inches, but it is now at the Devon Railway Centre at Bickleigh. The other two working locomotives were scrapped, as had been that bought for spares by 1969.

STANDARD-GAUGE LOCOMOTIVES

FORDSON

As the NDCJLR neared completion Henry Holwill realised a locomotive would be required to shunt the new standard-gauge connection. At Colonel Stephens' suggestion an order was placed for a Fordson petrol locomotive from Muir-Hill Engineering Ltd, of Manchester. Like the two-feet gauge versions at Meeth this was a conversion of a Fordson tractor, possibly with a separate rail chassis but perhaps simply with flanged wheels coupled by chains. It arrived in

MERSEY shunting between the exchange sidings and works.
R. W. KIDNER

June but after only a few days' trials it was found to have very little adhesion, and hence hauling power, and Muir-Hill were asked to take it away. The cost would have been £495 and it has been described as looking like a brake van. Subsequently sold to the Weston, Clevedon & Portishead Railway, it worked satisfactorily until closure of that line in 1940. It was said to be capable of hauling 75 tons there so perhaps it had been modified by Muir-Hill.

No 79
One of Andersons' engines was hired for £2.10s a week until the end of 1925 when it was bought for £150. An 0-6-0ST of Manning, Wardle's 'K' class and built in 1888, the locomotive had spent its working life on contracting work, starting on the Manchester Ship Canal where it was named Ardwick. Andersons' acquired it from the Rosyth Dockyard contract and, for £150, it must have been in poor condition when it reached Marland works. However, it sufficed for the limited work on the standard-gauge sidings, probably as second engine, until scrapped about 1946 after the first diesel arrived.

Mersey
In August 1925 *Mersey* was bought second-hand for £745 from dealers, Cudworth & Johnson of Wrexham, having been supplied new in 1892 to the Corporation of Birmingham. Later it had been at Lever Bros at Port Sunlight and presumably gained its name there. It was an 0-4-0ST, one of Black Hawthorn's standard designs, and lasted until scrapped in 1950, although its saddle-tank could be found about the works for some years afterwards.

Progress
1945 saw the first, and appropriately named, diesel at Marland. *Progress* was John Fowler's first locomotive of their class 400, of 60hp with mechanical transmission through a three-speed gearbox. In 1977, after problems due to its age had appeared, it was rebuilt at the works with a Leyland engine and Dowty Hydrostatic transmission, both second-hand from other works vehicles. The conversion was a success and the locomotive became the mainstay of the rail traffic, working daily, exchanging empty wagons for loaded ones between the loading bay and exchange siding. In case of breakdown, and

Standard gauge Fowler PROGRESS *at the works. May 1968.*
M. J. MESSENGER

as *Peter* could not be relied upon, a track was cleared alongside the sidings so a road vehicle could tow wagons with a wire rope. After closure of the rail link, along with the other two remaining diesels, it was preserved and now has a home at the Bodmin & Wenford Railway, in Cornwall.

Peter
An older Fowler was bought second-hand in May 1950 as a spare engine. It had formerly worked at a steel works in Newport, South Wales. For some years it was beyond use and stood in the engine shed unused but has subsequently been preserved in Cornwall, also at Bodmin.

Ruston & Hornsby diesel
When another locomotive was required as spare in place of *Peter*, like the narrow-gauge, the works turned to a Ruston & Hornsby product. A small 48hp four-wheeled diesel of Class 48DS was bought via dealers in 1975; previously it had been owned by Lec Refrigeration, at Bognor Regis. It too is now in Cornwall.

The first diesel at Marland, PROGRESS, *pausing between shunting.*
NORTH DEVON CLAY CO.

The three vans at the works, 1966. That with the extended wheelbase is in the centre. The perimeter seats are visible as are the steps fitted on to the doors.
M. J. MESSENGER

ROLLING STOCK

PASSENGER VEHICLES

From the outset workmen were carried on the railway as many lived at Torrington or en route, particularly at Yarde where the cottage row was built especially for them. They were originally conveyed in open wagons and the conversion to covered vans at some time was logical.

Three vans are known to have existed and two were simple conversions of ordinary wagons but the third had a very much longer wheelbase, about nine feet. No doubt all the conversion work was carried out by the works' carpenters and this latter wagon may have been specially built or was a 'stretching' of an ordinary wagon. The van bodies were simple and not very elegant additions to the open wagon body, with small windows to let in a little light. Wooden seats were provided around the perimeter. They were known as 'shanties' by the clay workers.

In 1909 a surprising purchase was made. The London County Council were sweeping away the horse trams of the capital with electrification and the cars of the former North Metropolitan Tramways Company became redundant in that year. Two were bought for workmen's transport and converted from standard-gauge. They were originally open-top double-deck cars seating about 36 but the staircases were removed and the platforms shortened at Marland at the same time as new buffing gear was fitted. Part of the knife-board, back-to-back seats remained on the roofs.

Who built these two cars is not readily apparent but they do differ in detail. About half the North Met's cars came from John Stephenson & Co. of New York and the one with the more prominently curving sides may be one of these. The other may have been built at the North Met's Leytonstone works or by one of the other British manufacturers, such as Hughes & Co. of Loughborough. At Marland one was painted yellow and the other blue, and each probably had seating for eighteen only.

After 1925 the tramcars were relegated to the moor to end their days as foreman's huts but their chilled iron wheels continued in use elsewhere, as it is reported they turned up from time to time at Hodges, in Exeter, for turning. The 'shanties' continued to carry workmen between a point close to Dunsbear Halt and the works, and between the works and the pits. One was intended to be preserved by a local school but was not. The wagon bought by the Seaton Tramway in East Devon was one of the short vans, without its van body, converted from one of the original Birmingham-built wagons.

Wagons

Fell turned to the Metropolitan Railway Carriage & Wagon Co. of Birmingham for the first wagons. Their drawing is dated 12 July 1880 and depicts a well designed four-wheel wagon intended to carry three tons. The body is ten feet long by five feet wide and carried on two-feet diameter wheels at a five feet six inches wheelbase. With a small side door they are very much miniature standard-gauge wagons; quite substantial and well engineered. A centre-buffer coupling is shown but as far as is known this was discarded in practice in favour of a centre buffer and side-chains. With one major alteration this style persisted for the next ninety years.

There is no record of how many wagons

One of the former horse-trams. The remains of the upper-deck seats can be clearly seen and the asymmetrical awning that formerly accommodated the staircase.
LOCOMOTIVE CLUB OF GREAT BRITAIN, KEN NUNN COLLECTION

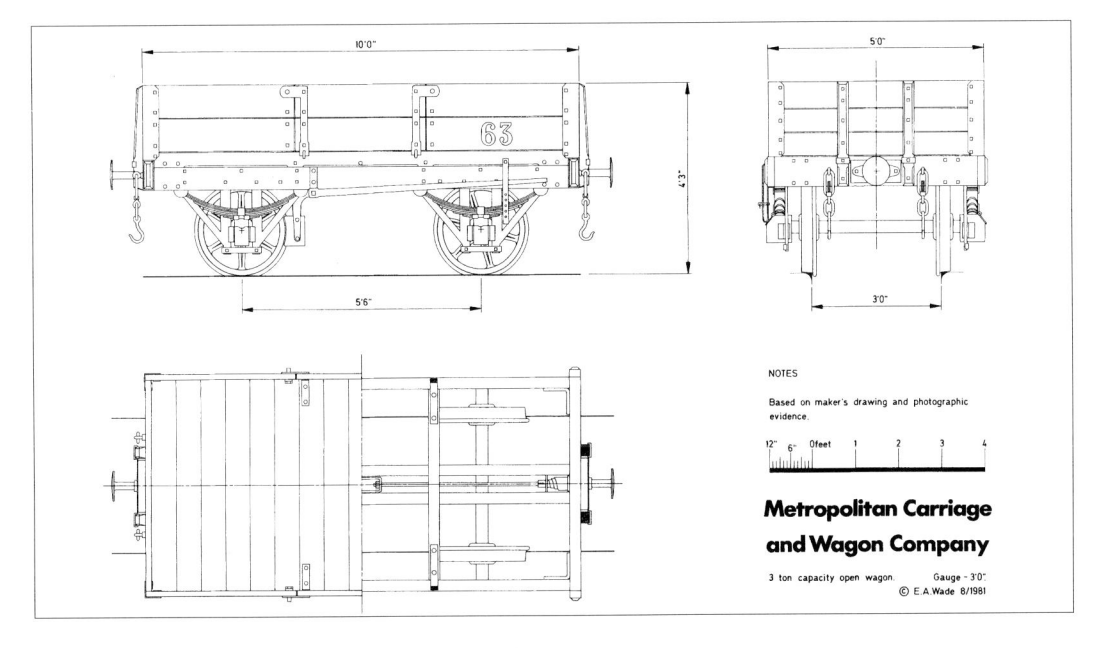

The carpenters' workshop at Marland works was well equipped and, amongst other things, built and maintained the fleet of railway wagons. This posed photograph shows a wagon underframe under construction.
NORTH DEVON CLAY CO.

were originally ordered but wagon numbers went up to at least 83. About 1893 there were 49, ten more were ordered in 1895 and another ten in 1901. The MRCW drawing also bears dates in 1910 and 1911 and these may indicate dates when quotations were given as the minute books make no further mention of orders. The Locomotive in 1913 states that there were nearly 100 wagons and that most were built at the works. Whilst the latter statement may not be strictly true it would seem that by then the works was in full charge of wagon manufacture and maintenance, with much of the metalwork - wheels, axles, axle boxes and brasses, springs and buffers - being supplied by Marcus Hodges, of Exeter. Wheels and axles also were regularly sent to Exeter for turning and re-profiling. This continued to the end and an unfinished chassis remained until at least 1981 in the carpenters' shop.

There were two types of wagon and the differences are apparent in photographs. The MRCW-built wagons had leaf springs, spoked wheels and a wheelbase of 5 feet 6 inches. They had a small side door. Those built at the works had coil springs, disc wheels and a wheelbase one foot shorter, to accommodate the curves around the pits. There are also differences in the end strapping and in the solebars; in the latter type they protruded beyond and across the ends of the buffer beams whereas in the former their length was contained within the buffer beams. Rebuilding blurred the distinctions between the two types, principally in the exchange of wheels and axleboxes. They were all painted light grey and numbered in a serif style of figure at the right-hand end. A wagon label clip was provided to indicate the grade of clay that the wagon was carrying. A report of 1962 suggests there were wagons of a longer, nine feet, wheelbase but there is no other evidence and surviving memories do not support it.

The Marland-built wagons had a full length drop side door, known as a 'lap' locally, and this enabled, after 1925 when the standard-gauge connection was made, the wagons' contents to be tipped bodily at the trans-shipment shed into standard-gauge wagons. After 1925 the older wagons were converted to full length drop side doors but not all had such doors on both sides. Some of the original MRCW wagons retained their small side door on one side, presumably for economy, and when the tipper was altered in the 1960s, tipping the opposite way, many wagons had to be turned for the new

Loaded wagons near the weigh-bridge. That on the left, number 83, is an original Birmingham built wagon, probably pre-1900, and the right-hand one, 32, was built at the works with a shorter wheelbase. The differences are readily apparent. May 1968.
M. J. MESSENGER

arrangements. It has been suggested that some of the locally-built wagons also only had a door on one side. A valuation of 1937 mentions 76 wagons, valued at £35 or £30 each, but by 1970 there were little more than 50 in all.

The other type of wagon in common use was a metal bodied side-tipping V-skip. These were used for removing waste clay and overburden for dumping and for taking sawdust from the sawmill, but not for the regular transport of the works as the metal would stain the clay. There were 14 in 1937 but reports in about 1962 suggest 20 to 30. Other wagons included flats for carrying machinery about the system and one with an air compressor mounted on it. Latterly one of the Jersey tenders survived. Pit props were carried in the normal wagons. In 1937 there were also two platelayers' trollies.

When closure came a wagon was bought by the Seaton & District Electric Tramway but the rest were burnt, shunted one by one into a gigantic bonfire. Seaton did not regauge their wagon and have since disposed of it.

Short two-foot and eighteen-inch gauge tracks also ran from the vicinity of the shafts to remove spoil and rubbish. On these ran standard tipping wagons which were known as 'Anderson' wagons, thus indicating their origin.

A former Jersey tender remained in use as a water tanker. The rivetted wrought-iron barrel could be a former locomotive boiler. July 1968.
B. D. HUGHES

NORTH DEVON CLAY

A close-up of a shaft-head showing wagons used at these locations. In the foreground is an eighteen-inch or two-foot gauge end tipping wagons for removing rubbish and behind is the shaft 'tub' for hauling clay out of the mine. NORTH DEVON CLAY CO.

A rather poor photograph of a standard gauge Gloucester Wagon Company built 10-ton wagon at Marland works. They proved unsuitable for the run to the Potteries and were used to take clay for shipment from Fremington. NORTH DEVON CLAY CO.

STANDARD-GAUGE WAGONS

The 1893 report states that nine standard-gauge wagons were then owned, although they could then get no closer to the works than Torrington. In the 1920s a number of standard-gauge wagons were hired from the Gloucester Wagon Company for Staffordshire traffic. They were former coal wagons with grease axle-boxes and of 10 ton capacity. If two trips a month to the Potteries were made the hire was economic as the rebate from the Southern Railway for 'owners wagons' was more than the wagon rental but trouble with axle boxes running hot restricted the wagons' availability and they were limited to the run between the clay works and Fremington before being discontinued. The 1937 valuation does not mention them.

CHAPTER SIX
STANDARD-GAUGE PROPOSALS

A quiet summer morning in August 1962, and an Ivatt Class 2 tank engine stands simmering gently in Petrockstow station, its single coach representing the morning train from Halwill to Torrington. It seems an age since it arrived, an arrival remarkable only for the rapid disappearance of the train crew, and now the only living things in sight are the solitary passenger and the station cat. The former calls to the latter who cordially strolls across the platform, obviously pleased to have some company, but soon the cat becomes bored with what is, after all, a one-sided conversation and goes to seek a more exciting distraction. The passenger too decides on a change of view and finding the driver, fireman and guard comfortably seated in the booking office enjoying a pot of tea, joins them until, refreshment complete, the train continues unhurriedly to Torrington.

Such was a not untypical journey by the writer on the North Devon & Cornwall Junction Light Railway but was this rural idyll really what the railway's promoters were seeking? This railway was the culmination of nearly one hundred years of activity and planning and its lethargy can only be described as an anti-climax.

The first proposal for a railway through this part of Devon was in 1831 when a line connecting Torrington and Okehampton was mooted. This would have commenced at the head of the Rolle Canal and run close beside the Torridge and Okement rivers to a terminus opposite the White Hart in Okehampton. Roger Hopkins, the engineer, had been responsible for the Plymouth & Dartmoor Railway and, later, for the Bodmin & Wadebridge Railway, and his report is full of detail. Although agricultural and coal traffic were the main targets, the carriage of pipe-clay and potters' clay also entered into Hopkins' calculations, along with timber, oak bark and granite. A branch line with an incline five furlongs long (1km) would have connected the limestone deposits in Okehampton Park.

The total length of the main-line would have been 18½ miles (30km) and the cost a little over £43,000. Hopkins envisaged a gauge of 4 feet 8 inches and two steam locomotives working three trips a day, but despite its general popularity this forward thinking scheme was not to be. It was prompted by the success of the Rolle Canal, opened 1825, but its logical development came with proposals for extension to Bideford, thus obviating the need for the newly cut canal and this may have led to opposition from Lord Rolle.

Much more ambitious was the proposed Bideford & Tavistock Railway of 1845, surveyed by Roger Hopkins' two sons, Rice and Thomas. Despite its title this line would have commenced at Sutton Pool, Plymouth, and run through Tavistock and Okehampton before following the 1831 route to Hatherleigh. From here it headed across Woolladon Moor to Bury Moor and Clay Moor, then taking the later narrow-gauge route to Torrington down the Pencleave Valley. After crossing the Torridge to Weare Gifford it was intended to run alongside the river through East-the-Water and Instow to make a junction at Fremington with the Taw Vale Railway before terminating by Barnstaple Bridge. The Bill failed to satisfy the standing orders of the House of Commons and a shorter scheme of 1852 did not even get this far.

The London & South Western Railway's protégé, the Okehampton Railway, later the Devon & Cornwall Central Railway, produced plans in 1864 and 1866 for lines to Bude and Torrington. It was to branch from the main-line near Sampford Courtenay and a short length of embankment appears to have been built, and only removed in the latter half of the twentieth century, but this was the only material progress. The line would have gone directly to Hatherleigh where the junction for Bude would have been, thence north-west through the clay lands to follow the stream to Torrington. It too was not built.

As the nineteenth century progressed the railway maps showed much of Britain well served by railways and the areas without such a facility grew in conspicuousness as they diminished in size. Such places attracted railway proposals in disproportion to their value and later reported comments suggest there were many other schemes for this corner of North Devon whose details have not survived.

The Langtree Lake stream that makes its way from Stowford Moor through Watergate and the Pencleave Valley to join the Torridge above Rothern Bridge, and which provides the parish boundary for most of the distance, was

65

Proposed Railways 1831-1895

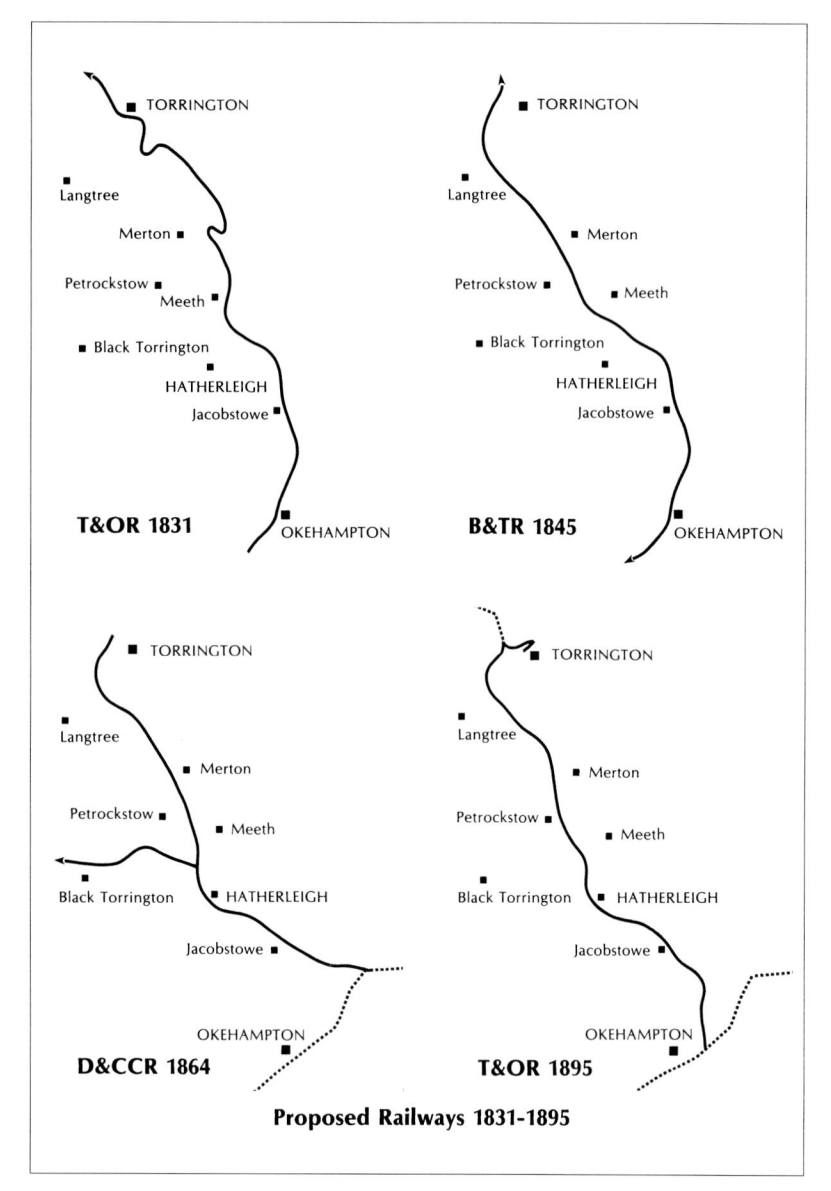

(Maps: T&OR 1831, B&TR 1845, D&CCR 1864, T&OR 1895, showing Torrington, Langtree, Merton, Petrockstow, Meeth, Black Torrington, Hatherleigh, Jacobstowe, Okehampton)

becoming well known to a number of railway engineers and surveyors, but it was J. B. Fell who eventually made use of it in 1880, as related in Chapter 3.

Whilst Fell's line satisfied the clay workings and the immediate vicinity, it did little for the area to the south, and the prosperous town of Hatherleigh in particular felt keenly the lack of a railway. In the 1890s several schemes were afoot to connect Torrington with the LSWR line to the south; Okehampton, Halwill, Sampford Courtenay and Holsworthy all being suggested as likely junctions. During November 1893 meetings were held in Holsworthy, Hatherleigh and Torrington and after all protagonists had put their own ideas forward, and these included light and narrow-gauge railways, a route to a point near Okehampton was settled upon.

Great hopes were held out for tourist traffic between North Devon and North Cornwall, coal from Fremington to Okehampton, Plymouth and other towns, business traffic between North and South Devon, expansion of the Marland clay works, the Hatherleigh brickworks and the Hatherleigh stone quarries. A prospectus for the Torrington & Okehampton Railway, issued in 1896 following an 1895 Act, estimated 60,000 passengers, 35,000 tons of coal, manure and goods and 30,000 tons of clay, bricks and pottery, each year. Needless to say they expected a profit, of over 7½%. A particular point made was the saving of at least 30 miles between Torrington or Bideford and towns to the south.

The authorised capital of the T&OR was £250,000 and an additional £83,333 could be borrowed on mortgage. The directors were nearly all from Bideford and the engineer was James T. Jervis, who later engineered the Bideford, Westward Ho! & Appledore Railway. Whilst the LSWR had declined to build the railway they had agreed to work it when complete for 50% of the gross receipts. An interesting point in the Act was that the line could be built as a light railway if wished.

The 20½ mile (33km) route was to take that of the narrow-gauge line out of Torrington up the Pencleave Valley continuing past Petrockstow, Hatherleigh and Jacobstowe to join the LSWR main-line at Fatherford, east of Okehampton. The North Devon Clay Co. petitioned against the 1895 Bill on the grounds that their narrow-gauge line satisfied all their requirements but withdrew this following the insertion of clauses protecting their interests and the payment of £1,000 deposit for the narrow-gauge route. The NDCC were concerned at the possibility of losing their economical transport and having to pay full commercial rates on a line that they did not ask for.

The T&OR made rather slow progress and it is clear they had difficulty raising the necessary capital as meetings to promote the railway were held as far away as Plymouth and Devonport. An extension of time to build the railway was sought from Parliament in 1898 and again the NDCC petitioned against the Bill, this time on the grounds that the T&OR should get on and build the railway, and remove the uncertainty from the project.

Clay production had dropped on the formation of the NDCC but was picking up very well in the mid-1890s, and traffic on the light railway had increased considerably, perhaps doubling. With the spectre of the line's replacement about to appear the Company did not wish to spend money on it but the heavier traffic was calling for expenditure on maintenance and improvement. A further bone of contention was the free workmen's trains which cost very little to run as part of the mineral services but fares on the proposed railway would be £300 to £500 a year. Furthermore, the Company could not afford to have its lifeline severed during construction of the T&OR.

The legal wrangles took six years and it was not until 1901 that agreement was reached. Possibly these troubles may have delayed the T&OR as much as their lack of money but when agreement came they were no nearer building their railway. In 1900 this state of affairs had come to the notice of *The Financial Times* who, in a long scathing article headed 'Devonian Drollery', commented:

> The primary function of a railway company is to possess a railway, but the Torrington and Okehampton Railway Company has been in existence some years, and neither possesses a yard of track, nor appears to have the slightest prospect of doing so in the near future. To atone for this disappointing state of affairs the Directors do their utmost to make the annual report a exceedingly humorous document, and in this effort they achieve no inconsiderable success. We are not surprised, however, to find that the shareholders are dissatisfied; they provided capital (to a very limited amount) for the construction of a railway, and are disappointed to find that they have secured no more for their money than a life subscription to a comic annual.

The paper pointed out that of the £¼m required only £24,120 was subscribed, of which £15,764 had been called up. The balance sheet showed assets of book value of £10,346 and liabilities of over £16,000, while the capital account stood at the magnificent sum of £8.11s.2d. It was recommended that the shareholders insist upon the liquidation of the company and that the directors

> return to their aldermanic and magisterial duties before their self-complacency is disturbed by the unpleasant consequences of their monumental stupidity.

What appeared to be quite good advice was not heeded and in 1901 a further Act was obtained for another extension of time and the name of the scheme was changed to the Plymouth & North Devon Direct Railway. This example of cosmetic nomenclature achieved little and in September Lord Clinton was reported as saying the railway would never be made. Although early in 1902 a firm of railway contractors, J. B. Squire & Co. of London, said they were expecting instructions any day they never received them and in 1907 the proposals were legally abandoned by yet another Act of Parliament.

The local people, again, were the sufferers for they lost the money they had subscribed but may actually have been better off without a railway. Quite what effect the various proposals would have had on the district, had any been successful, is hard to gauge but it is likely that they would not have been entirely beneficial. Although the clay industry would have gained, the benefit of good communication was a double-edged blade in many country communities. The ease with which factory products could be imported caused the closure of many rural industries and the railway then took away the new unemployed and the poorly paid labourer to work in the towns, thus hastening the depopulation of the countryside, with decreasing profitability for the railway as a result.

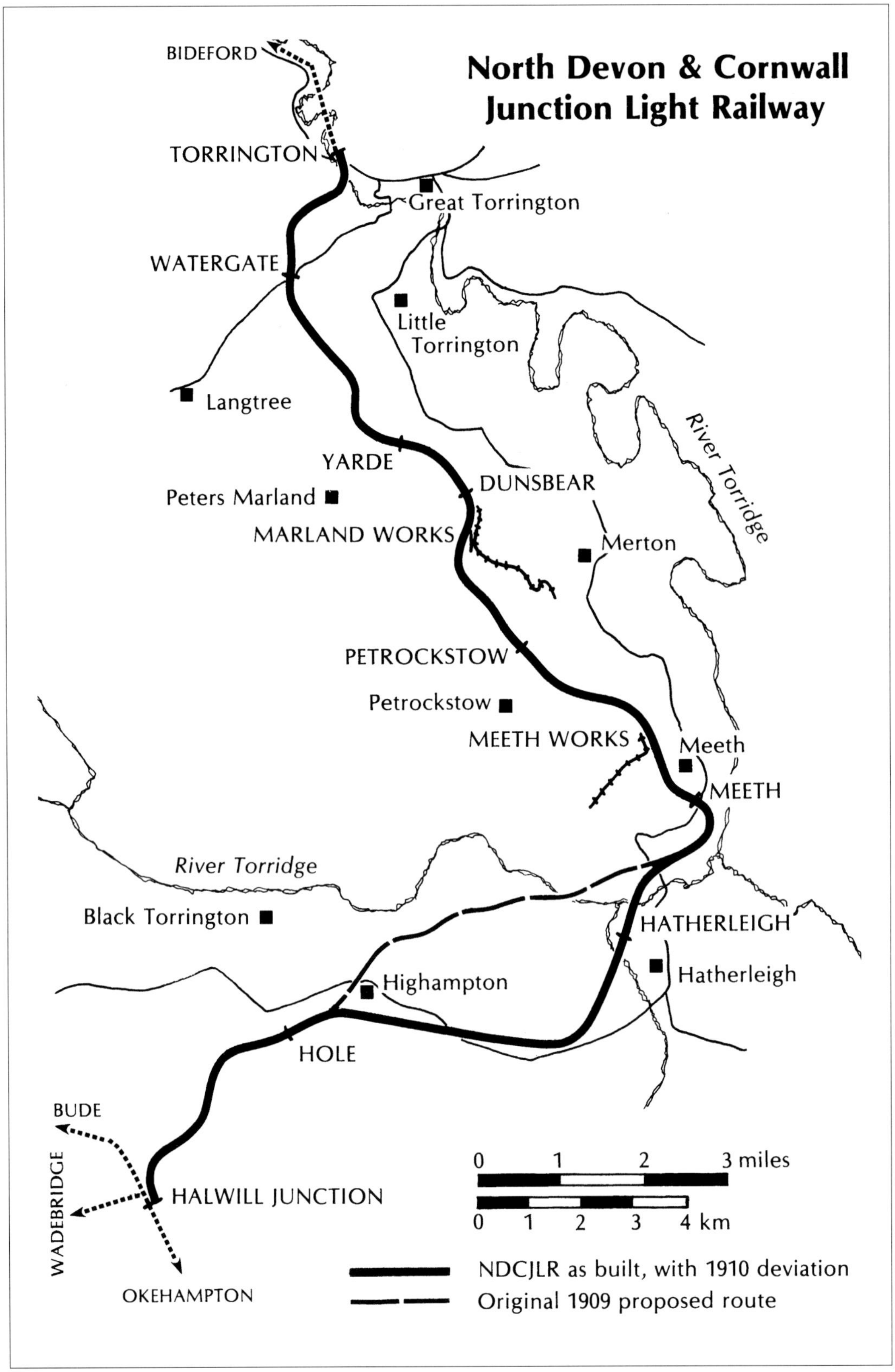
North Devon & Cornwall Junction Light Railway
BIDEFORD
TORRINGTON
Great Torrington
WATERGATE
Little Torrington
Langtree
River Torridge
YARDE
DUNSBEAR
Peters Marland
MARLAND WORKS
Merton
PETROCKSTOW
Petrockstow
MEETH WORKS
Meeth
MEETH
River Torridge
Black Torrington
HATHERLEIGH
Hatherleigh
Highampton
HOLE
BUDE
WADEBRIDGE
HALWILL JUNCTION
OKEHAMPTON
0 1 2 3 miles
0 1 2 3 4 km
NDCJLR as built, with 1910 deviation
Original 1909 proposed route

CHAPTER SEVEN
THE NORTH DEVON & CORNWALL JUNCTION LIGHT RAILWAY

In 1909 a Mr Stephens came upon the scene with yet another proposal, but his ideas differed in certain aspects. Holman Fred Stephens was without doubt the most ardent champion of light railways in Great Britain. Born in 1868, after studying in Civil Engineering at University College London he embarked on a career in railways and whilst in his early twenties commenced projecting and promoting light railways. He was elected an Associate Member of the Institute of Civil Engineers in 1894.

Like Fell he saw the economically built and operated light railway as the means to cheap rural transport. Light railways needed to be built with the minimum of formalities without the onerous rules applicable to main-line railways and to be able to work with the maximum of flexibility to serve the local community adequately. Parliament had half-heartedly legislated in 1868 to meet this need but not a great deal was achieved, although Devon in particular benefited. In 1896 the Light Railways Act was passed and this encouraged the promotion of many light railways throughout the United Kingdom.

Stephens was already controlling half-a-dozen such lines, mainly in South East England, when, by some means now unknown, he conceived the idea of a light railway in North Devon. His initial letter to the NDCC dated 24 May 1909 sought their response to a suggested use of their railway for part of the route, laying down a third rail to accommodate standard-gauge. This ingenious idea lapsed when he found the Torridge Viaduct would not take the weight of a standard-gauge truck let alone a train. In August he visited the area to take a trip on the narrow-gauge line and by November plans were sufficiently advanced for an application to be made to the Light Railway Commissioners for a Light Railway Order.

An example of the hectic life Stephens led can be seen in a meeting he had with the NDCC directors on 2 February 1910 when he arrived at Bideford at 3.10pm and left again on the 5.26pm train. In order to meet him the directors held their board meeting in the waiting room on the down platform of Bideford station.

A point of dispute was the purchase price of the Marland Railway. The NDCC were asking £25,000 for the route and the track of the line but Stephens thought this too much and when he suggested he would make a separate line alongside to Torrington, leaving them untouched, Henry Holwill threatened to oppose

Holman Fred Stephens

Anderson's Hudswell Clarke 0-4-0ST, BIRKENHEAD, tipping to form an embankment somewhere on the new line.
BEAFORD CENTRE

Builders of railways in the twentieth century had the benefit of substantial mechanised equipment like this Ruston steam excavator, seen here loading BUNTY's train of M.S.C. wagons. It was not included in Anderson's sale so may have been hired.
BEAFORD CENTRE

GYP engaged in filling in a timber viaduct, probably Yarde. The distinctive design of Fell's viaduct can be seen clearly.
BEAFORD CENTRE

the Order. A figure of £18,000 was eventually agreed upon, although afterwards Stephens frequently complained at this.

The Light Railway Commissioners held their enquiry at Torrington on 28 February 1910 and many local people gave evidence of the need for a railway through the district, and particularly to Hatherleigh. In addition to clay there would be considerable agricultural traffic, especially cattle and hay. Stephens estimated the cost at £133,053, almost half that of the T&OR. This included £20,000 for a new Torridge Viaduct. The promoters were James Oag, JP, a director of the North Cornwall Railway, H. F. Stephens on behalf of himself and 'some financial friends in London interested in light railways' and Mr

A newly built Meeth Halt with unconsolidated track and an unfinished platform. Behind is Anderson's other Manning Wardle 0-6-0ST 244 and a number of two-foot gauge wagons.
LOCOMOTIVE PUBLISHING COMPANY

Rylett, a contractor. They claimed not to be relying on local money but had access to funds apparently, and also had in mind obtaining grants and loans from the Treasury and local authorities.

One large local landowner, J. C. Moore Stevens, opposed the plans but a deviation to miss his home farm was devised and he was appeased, eventually to become a director of the railway company and an enthusiastic supporter. A few other local people had objections but it was felt that these could be overcome, in the cause of the common good, and the Commissioners approved the application. Their report, brief but in favour, was not issued until January 1913 and the Order was published the following year. In the meantime Devon County Council had been persuaded to subscribe £15,000 and Holsworthy, Okehampton and Torrington Rural District Councils £5,000 each.

The North Devon & Cornwall Junction Light Railway Order 1914 incorporated the company of the same name and authorised the construction and operation of the railway. Detailed speed restrictions were incorporated, and limits as to weight of rails and rolling stock. Clauses protected the rights of the NDCC, the local authorities and the LSWR. Motive power was to be steam without the Board of Trade's consent for anything else.

The route was to follow the Torrington & Marland Railway, as far as Dunsbear, whence it took a new line to the west of Marland works crossing Marland Moor and Bury Moor on higher ground to avoid the clay beds. Similarly Stockleigh Moors and Woolladon Moor were skirted to the east and the line headed towards the River Torridge, which it followed for a mile or so. The original route would have kept close to the Torridge until Brembridge when it would have cut across country to Highampton but a deviation of 1910 took the route nearer Hatherleigh by following the River Lew and the Pulworthy Brook to Highampton. From here it was a straight-forward run across country to Halwill. Even after the deviation the proposed Hatherleigh station, at Lewer Bridge, was not very convenient for the town and caused some adverse comment. The line was to be 20¼ miles (32.5km) long.

In July 1914 an application was made for a Treasury grant of £30,000 and a further loan of a like sum as the Board of Agriculture had certified that the line would be a benefit to agriculture. The NDCC had agreed to take part of their £18,000 in shares and debentures and Stephens spent much time trying to increase the proportion of shares, not very successfully. Raising finance, once again, looked like being the hurdle that the railway could not get over but it was events in Europe, of far greater importance than transport problems down in Devon, that caused all scheming to be suspended.

At first it was hoped that the railway would proceed as an unemployment relief scheme but in North Devon immediately after the outbreak of the Great War there was no unemployment and the Treasury advised Stephens to withdraw his application for a grant until after hostilities had ceased. At this time some 105,000 tons of freight were estimated as likely traffic giving a total income of £25,330 per annum.

By October 1914 H. F. Stephens was

Petrockstow station, almost complete, but awaiting signalling. What appears to be an inspection party is on the platform.
LOCOMOTIVE PUBLISHING COMPANY

Assistant Chief Engineer to Kitchener's Third Army with the rank of Lieutenant Colonel and was having difficulty running his personal railway empire with but 48 hours leave a week. Surprisingly, in response to a query from Henry Holwill who had spotted the General Manager and Chief Engineer of the LSWR looking over the route of the proposed line, twelve months later he was able to write:

> We are still at work on the ND&CJR but there is no chance of getting any money yet ... the line will be started ... as soon as any other public work in the Country is started.

During the war years the Light Railway Order's powers were kept alive by the Board of Trade under emergency regulations and in October 1918 the now Colonel Stephens wrote to Henry Holwill 'We mean having a good try for the ND&CJR as soon as the crisis is over.' A poignant and personal note entered the correspondence between the two men at this time when Henry Holwill referred to the death of his younger son as a prisoner-of-war in Germany. Colonel Stephens replied that he had lost half of his friends - 'the best go first'.

After the War David Lloyd George's Government set about establishing a policy for transport matters and a Ministry of Ways and Communications was proposed. This became fact as the Ministry of Transport and its first Minister was Sir Eric Campbell Geddes. On 17 March 1919 he made a lengthy policy speech in the House of Commons in which light railways were briefly mentioned. Sir Eric, formerly Deputy General Manager of the North Eastern Railway, had been Director-General of Military Railways to the Army during the Great War, later Inspector-General of Transportation, and probably knew more about light railways and their value than most politicians. He thought little of Britain's existing lines and thought roads were more suitable for their traffic: 'I think that we must look to the development of motor traction for our agricultural areas'. In response Hatherleigh Parish Council wrote urging their need for a railway and pointing out that the local roads were not in a fit state to take the traffic.

1919 saw an intensive campaign of canvassing support for the NDCJLR, both moral and financial, of and by local Councillors and Members of Parliament, with no small success. Devon County Council increased their promised assistance to £40,000 and Torrington Rural District Council to £12,000, while Barnstaple and Bideford Town Councils offered £2,000 and £1,000 respectively. The Government, however, were embarrassed by Colonel Stephens' request for a grant or loan from central funds as they had no policy for such matters. Some help was certainly needed for the cost had shot up to an estimated £292,000, although Stephens thought he could manage with £220,000 and sought an interest-free government loan of £100,000. A rival scheme to build a line to Okehampton instead of Halwill was soon scotched.

In April 1920 a government survey party was despatched to North Devon to examine the proposals and the area's needs. This they did in some considerable detail. Production of the North Devon Clay Company Ltd and the embryo Meeth (North Devon) Clay Company was detailed, as was the agricultural produce (2,150 milk churns, for example) and all interested local people were interviewed. We learn that Hatherleigh market dealt with £250,000-worth of cattle and sheep per year and that 2,000 tons of hay were sold annually. A population of 13,000 in 17 parishes and 62,935 acres (98 square miles) would be served. The Board of Trade, Ministry of Agriculture and Timber Supply Department were consulted, and so were the LSWR. Sir Herbert Walker, the LSWR General Manager, agreed there was a need for a light railway but stated it could not be made to pay and his company would need a guarantee of 100% of the gross receipts before they agreed to work the line.

The main parts of the resultant report were written by H. H. Holbrook, one-time Superintendent of the Line on the Liskeard & Looe Railway, and he certainly favoured a light railway:

> No road motor service would satisfactorily deal with the traffic of the district. The need for a light railway was apparent and justified. A railway of standard-gauge constructed in the simplest manner with siding accommodation at road crossings, and worked as a tramway with frequent stopping places, would best meet the needs of the district.

J. Ferguson, Civil Engineer, said it should be regarded as a pioneer line, built simply and to be improved later when traffic warranted it. He suggested it be laid with 60 lb rail, unfenced and with a speed limit of 20 mph.

The survey party were evidently in favour of the scheme and it moved on for consideration at a higher level. In October the Treasury declined to provide £180,000 but the following month came an indication that up to £125,000 might be found. The wheels of Government, as ever, ground exceedingly slowly, and in March 1921 the Cabinet deferred a decision until the new Chancellor could examine it but in the meantime another factor was appearing, to be a strong influence on the decision makers. This was rising unemployment in post-War Britain. A Cabinet Committee on Unemployment was

Old and new viaducts. On the opening day of the NDCJLR, 27 July 1925, Fell's viaduct is now disconnected and waits demolition having been replaced by the standard gauge viaduct on the right.
H. C. CASSERLEY

Construction work somewhere on the NDCJLR, probably south of Petrockstowe as there is no sign of the three-foot gauge Torrington & Marland. Two-foot gauge track and Jubilee wagons are in use here.
BEAFORD CENTRE

formed and Hatherleigh Parish Council, ever eager for the chance to promote the railway, wrote to Dr Macnamara, Minister of Labour, drawing attention to the NDCJLR as a scheme to relieve the unemployed. A month later, in October, Colonel Stephens was able to write 'I am rather more hopeful than usual (if we can only keep the politicians out of it)'.

His sentiments were ill-founded for the NDCJLR had become a political animal. A Light Railways (Investigation) Committee had made a number of recommendations to make other light railways considered of more value but the Ministry of Transport were anxious for a railway to be built to test their new policies on rural transport. The Ministry of Labour needed a construction project to relieve unemployment and above all the Treasury sat brooding over the public purse strings.

To add to these problems there was competition for Government support from at least six other proposals although the NDCJLR was the most advanced and occupied the highest position in the priority list. The other schemes were in West Somerset, Gower (2), the Lleyn Peninsular, Lincolnshire and Yorkshire. Much of the closing months of 1921 were spent fund-raising to maintain this priority for the Government were only likely to match local investment pound for pound. It was reported that more than 14 parishes had subscribed £18,320 and the Rector of Pyworthy subscribed £100 himself. The *Western Morning News* offered £500 from their unemployment fund on condition 100 men were taken on, preferably ex-servicemen.

William Balsdon, a Hatherleigh grocer and farmer, who was also Chairman of the Meeth (North Devon) Clay Co. Ltd, played a considerable part in the fund-raising exercise and both he and Colonel Stephens spent some time persuading Henry Holwill to accept as much as possible of the £18,000 purchase price for the Torrington & Marland Railway in shares and debentures instead of cash. Eventually agreement was reached to take £14,000 in this manner. Balsdon later claimed to have written over a thousand letters in support of the railway scheme.

At the first Board Meeting of the NDCJLR, on 16 February 1922, it was noted that the £125,000 had been raised, £85,580 was from local authorities, £34,926 came from other sources, mainly in the manner of financing land and material purchase, and the Meeth (North Devon) Clay Co. Ltd. had offered to guarantee the balance of £4,494.

The LSWR had agreed - perhaps after official pressure - to work the line for 75% of the gross receipts with a minimum payment to the NDCJLR of £6,500, enough to pay the 5% interest on the debentures. At last on 23 March 1922 agreement was signed with the Ministry of Transport who agreed to subscribe £125,000, or half the cost if less, taking equal amounts of ordinary shares and debenture stock. The most important condition was that unskilled labour was to be used in the construction and drawn from areas designated by the Ministry of Labour. Tenders were sought from contractors for the work and initially McAlpine's was accepted but it was withdrawn and in due course the contract was awarded to P. & W. Anderson Ltd, of Glasgow, the cheapest at £197,000.

The first sod was ceremoniously cut at Lewer Bridge, near Hatherleigh, on 30 June 1922 by Arthur Neal MP, Parliamentary Secretary to the Minister of Transport, who received a silver cigarbox for his trouble. At the ensuing lunch at the Manor Hall a message from the Minister of Labour was read in which he said the railway would be 'a boon to those men who honestly wanted work'. What a prophetic remark that was to prove.

Andersons began moving men and machinery into the area and construction soon started, commencing at the Halwill end initially. In September Holwill consented to them using the T&MR, either with their own rolling stock or the North Devon Clay Co.'s. An important proviso was that clay traffic was to have priority at all times and it was a condition of the agreement with Stephens that the work would not sever the three-foot gauge railway. This was to cause a number of problems but seems to have been achieved most of the time.

The resident engineer was Captain J. H. T. Griffiths who had a base at 9 Bridge Street, Hatherleigh, with two junior engineers and three assistants. One of the assistants, Humphrey Brandram-Jones, later recorded his memories of this employment, his first after graduating. He recalls how the whole project was run on a shoestring. The railway was to run through a remote rural area and the works were far from decent roads, in a continual sea of mud, so getting about was difficult. Captain Griffiths had the use of a 680cc Sunbeam motor-cycle with sidecar but the others had to rely on one large, and apparently uncomfortable, horse. Colonel Stephens on his inspection visits travelled in a chauffeur-driven lorry, which came with a set of flanged wheels. By fitting these the Colonel could visit quickly any part of the works that rails had been laid to.

Little notice seems to have been taken of the requirement to use the unemployed on the construction, a point that Andersons no doubt wished to avoid if possible, for in December 1922 the *Western Morning News* threatened to cancel their subscription. By the following spring some move towards correcting this had been made, although the contractor was making it clear that they were not a charity. However, local people were becoming concerned at the conditions the men were living in. What was the norm and accepted for construction workers' accommodation during the nineteenth century was not so, apparently, in the new post-Great War twentieth-century Britain. Brandram-Jones recalls labourers sleeping in roughly constructed shelters near where they were working. A number of huts were provided by the contractors but not as many as promised and tents were proposed. Whether the huts were of adequate quality was a matter of opinion and these certainly differed. Bideford Council complained to the Ministry of Labour and local MP Basil Peto was sent to investigate. Another local MP, George Lambert, raised the matter in

Construction workers at Hatherleigh, 1925.
BEAFORD CENTRE

Beside the Torridge Viaduct Anderson have commenced work. Piers for the new viaduct are just above ground level. Standard gauge and two-foot gauge construction railways are apparent.
E. A. HOLWILL

the House, stating housing and conditions were 'not consistent with decent standards'. There were supposed to be plenty of lodgings available but local people were taking advantage of the situation and were charging 22s. to 25s. for a week's board and lodge. It was said that men would not take the work because they could not, in effect, afford to maintain two homes. The Bishop of Crediton opened a voluntary fund to provide shelters for the men and although the 'scandal' occupied much of 1923 it seems to have been resolved thereafter.

Poor weather during the winter of 1922/23 had held up the work but labour presented other problems that also delayed matters. Unlike professional navvies that Andersons preferred to employ those from the dole queues were not fit enough for the arduous work; some had been office workers or professional men. The conditions were bad and the work hard for those not used to it or to a fifty-plus hour week, and the men would not stay on the construction works.

Not all men who did stay wanted to work or intended to stay for very long as an incident on 23 June 1923 was to show, It was also to give the town of Hatherleigh a topic of conversation for many a day afterwards. A gang of 20 unemployed men had recently arrived from the Barbican in Plymouth and, as had become customary among the workers, adjourned to the town on Saturday afternoon to relax after the week's work. This particular group had other ideas as well as a few hours drinking.

Dancing in the street to the town band was innocent enough but when the band stopped at 9.45pm the men moved into the pubs. Half an hour later a group of 30 or 40 had gathered in the Square and were becoming rowdy. When they commenced singing 'The Red Flag' Sergeant Babb suggested it was time they returned to camp. A scuffle ensued in which the sergeant was knocked to the ground several times and was probably saved from being killed by PC W. J. Hutchings who stood over him fighting off the crowd amidst a hail of bottles, sticks and stones. Several townspeople came to the aid of the two policemen - among the first was C. J. Channon, manager of the Meeth clay works - and they were quickly followed by some of the 'regular' navvies, who had no love for the workshy. After the fracas it was found that the men had brought surgical bandages with them in anticipation of trouble.

Several arrests were made and sentences of up to five months hard labour were handed out later. Hatherleigh was rather indignant about the affair; not so much because the town's peace had been disrupted but because of the attack on their two police officers, who were well respected, both by the townspeople and the genuine navvies. Sergeant Babb had been in the town for ten years and Constable Hutchings was noted for his prowess as a boxer, fortunately in the event. PC Hutchings later wrote the official history of the Devon Constabulary and in this he recounts how he and Sergeant Babb had a high opinion of the genuine navvies who he describes as 'men of destiny, strong and rough, but honest and loyal to any good cause'. The police station acted as a centre for men arriving looking for accommodation, with a supply of cast-off clothing and a meal for those in need.

The professional navvy found his danger in his work. William Boundy, a 51 year old who had been with Andersons on several contracts, died in May 1923 when he fell out of a derailed wagon and was run over. Another unfortunate death was that of Andersons' pay clerk. Unable to account for a £1,200 shortfall in his cash he drowned himself in a quarry near Halwill Junction. Sadly the 'discrepancy' was merely a misunderstanding.

A further Light Railway Order was obtained in 1922 to increase the capital of the railway company to £260,000 and to authorise the government subsidy. In 1923, due to the delays in construction, another had to be obtained to authorise an extension of time. The purpose of this was evidently not generally made known and several local authorities initially objected to the Order.

Wet weather prevailed for much of the second half of the year and winter floods undermined one of the new viaduct's piers in the Torridge. It should have been demolished and rebuilt but was winched back upright and underpinned. Apart from that work continued rather less eventfully during 1924 but early in 1925 the next problem arose. In February a Mr Maloney was appointed Receiver and Manager of P. & W. Anderson Ltd. Whether it was the troubles and difficulties of building the NDCJLR that brought financial disaster to the contractors is not known. The Receiver continued the contract for two or three weeks after which Colonel Stephens continued the work, controlling it himself and employing labour direct, utilising the contractor's plant. From April the Colonel was able to take the occasional load of clay from the Meeth company's siding to Halwill. It was not until late May, when the Torridge Viaduct was by-passed, that he was able to do the same for the Marland works, although this was a matter of obligation rather than the favour Meeth received. The former had to have their clay carried to Torrington, if they could not use their own three-feet gauge railway, but the Meeth people suffered from a very indifferent and intermittent service that ran very much at the Colonel's convenience. Andersons' locomotives had been very poorly maintained and were barely adequate for the construction purposes, let alone hauling clay.

The LSWR had by now been grouped into the Southern Railway who assumed their responsibilities for the NDCJLR. The Southern would not permit the contractor's engines to work into Torrington station so trains had to be propelled from Marland works and preceded by a 15-ton goods brake van because of the gradients. In early July the Southern commenced working the traffic with their own engines and crews, presumably in order to test the new line and to train the staff who would be working it. By July 1925 the railway was sufficiently complete to enable Major C. L. Hall of the Ministry of Transport to inspect it on the 17th and he found little serious to criticise. The small defects were insufficient to delay opening the line and sanction was duly given.

Anderson's 79 was eventually bought by the North Devon Clay Co. when the construction work finished. Here it is still in Anderson's hands with sprung buffers removed and blocks suitable for contractors wagons fitted.
BEAFORD CENTRE

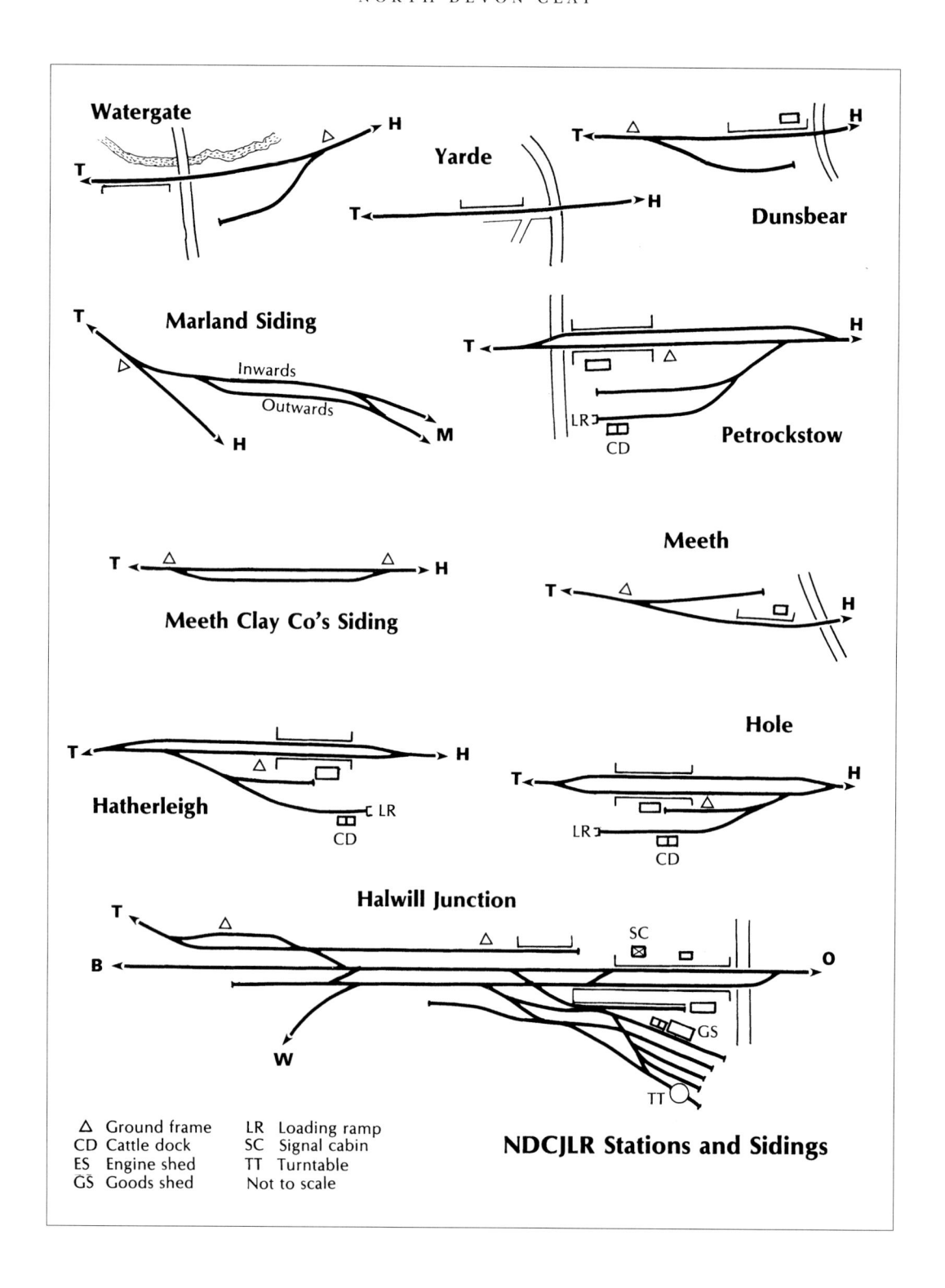

NORTH DEVON CLAY

Watergate

Yarde

Dunsbear

Marland Siding

Inwards
Outwards

Petrockstow

Meeth

Meeth Clay Co's Siding

Hole

Hatherleigh

Halwill Junction

△ Ground frame
CD Cattle dock
ES Engine shed
GS Goods shed
LR Loading ramp
SC Signal cabin
TT Turntable
Not to scale

NDCJLR Stations and Sidings

CHAPTER EIGHT
A SOUTHERN BRANCH LINE

With a complete absence of ceremony, on 27 July 1925 the North Devon & Cornwall Junction Light Railway opened for public service and, typically of many west country openings, it poured with rain. Some eighty people, mainly clay workers, joined the first train from Torrington at 6.30am. Amongst them was Torrington's mayor, George Doe, who had the first ticket, as he did from Bideford in 1872. The Halwill correspondent of the *Okehampton Post* approved of the saloon type coach, which gave good views, but complained a lot of time was wasted at Halwill as the engine had to cross the main-line to turn and take water. He would also have preferred the service to be run from the Halwill end so an earlier start could be made from there.

The following Thursday saw an opening ceremony when representatives of the local authorities and landowners were treated by Colonel Stephens to luncheon at Hatherleigh station. Given the size of the station it could not have been a very large function.

At last Hatherleigh and the surrounding villages had the standard-gauge railway they had so long coveted and by far the most interesting and exciting part of the railway's story was complete. As intimated earlier, the story of the functioning railway is rather bland and pedestrian in comparison with its genesis.

Major Hall's report gives an excellent description of the completed 20½ mile line. The track, laid on native oak and creosoted redwood sleepers on local stone ballast, was second-hand LSWR 87lb rail, worn to 84lb per yard. On the new route few curves were less than 20 chains (440 yards - 403m) radius and no gradient was more than 1 in 50, but on the old Marland line curves were as sharp as 9 chains (198 yards - 181m) and gradients as steep as 1 in 45 and 1 in 42, although the original line had been much worse.

There were 24 bridges, over and under the line, plus the new Torridge Viaduct, which had nine spans of 60 feet (18m) on the square or 55½ feet skew. Most of the bridges were cattle creeps but girder bridges crossed the Rolle Road (30 feet skew span), the main road north of Hatherleigh (28 feet skew), the River Torridge (two 66 feet spans) and the River Lew (40 feet span).

The line was particularly well endowed with level crossings; nine of public roads, 81 occupation crossings, four footpaths and one bridle path. The roads were protected by cattle guards, notices and a 10 m.p.h. speed restriction for 200 yards on each side.

Passing loops were at Petrockstow (24 wagons), Hatherleigh (21) and Hole (22) and these stations were the block posts with the electric tablet equipment (Tyers No 6) by which the line was worked. The station buildings were of a standard design and each had a men's lavatory, goods store, waiting room, booking office and general store. In addition to a seven-lever frame and a verandah (34½ feet by 6 feet) the equipment was completed by oil lamps and a coke stove. Apart from Petrockstow, which was 200 feet (61m) long, all platforms on the line were 167 feet (51m) long.

Two lesser stations, with no loop and only one platform at each, were Dunsbear and Meeth and they sported simple buildings incorporating waiting room, goods store and office. Like the other station buildings they had rubble walling and asbestos tile roofs. Sidings were provided at Watergate, Dunsbear, Marland (NDCC), Meeth Clay Co., and Meeth Halt, in addition to those at the passing stations. Up was towards Torrington, Halwill being regarded as the outwards terminal.

At Halwill Junction the NDCJLR was kept at

This is said to be the first train on the NDCJLR but it must be the return working. LSWR 4-4-0 No.475E at Hatherleigh. 27 July 1925.
BEAFORD CENTRE

Torrington 1950s

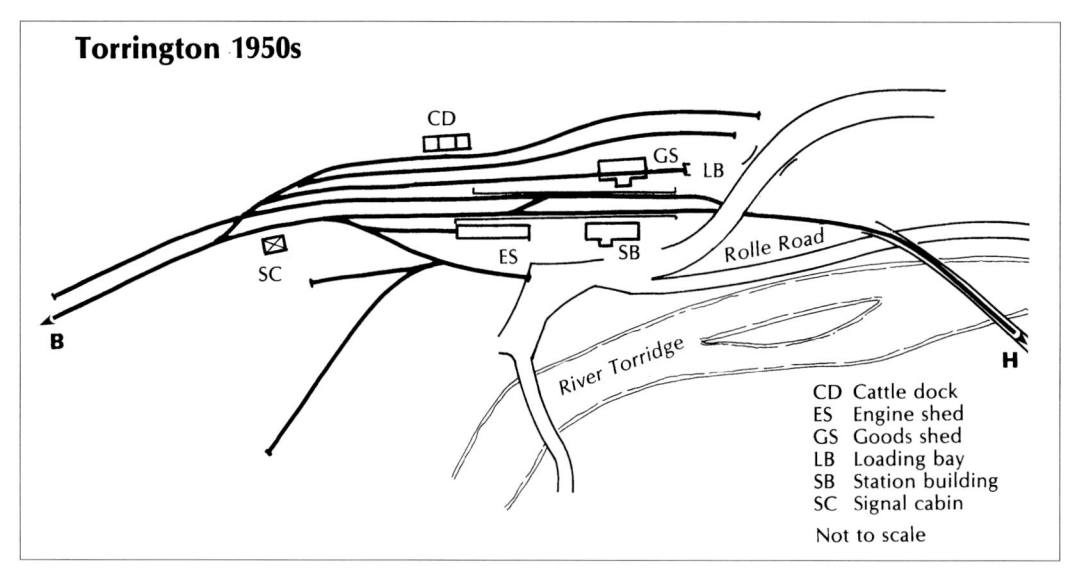

CD Cattle dock
ES Engine shed
GS Goods shed
LB Loading bay
SB Station building
SC Signal cabin

Not to scale

a respectable distance with a peculiar bay platform of its own at the Bude end of the up platform, adding another facet to the unique character of this hub of intermittent activity, where trains from four directions now briefly met.

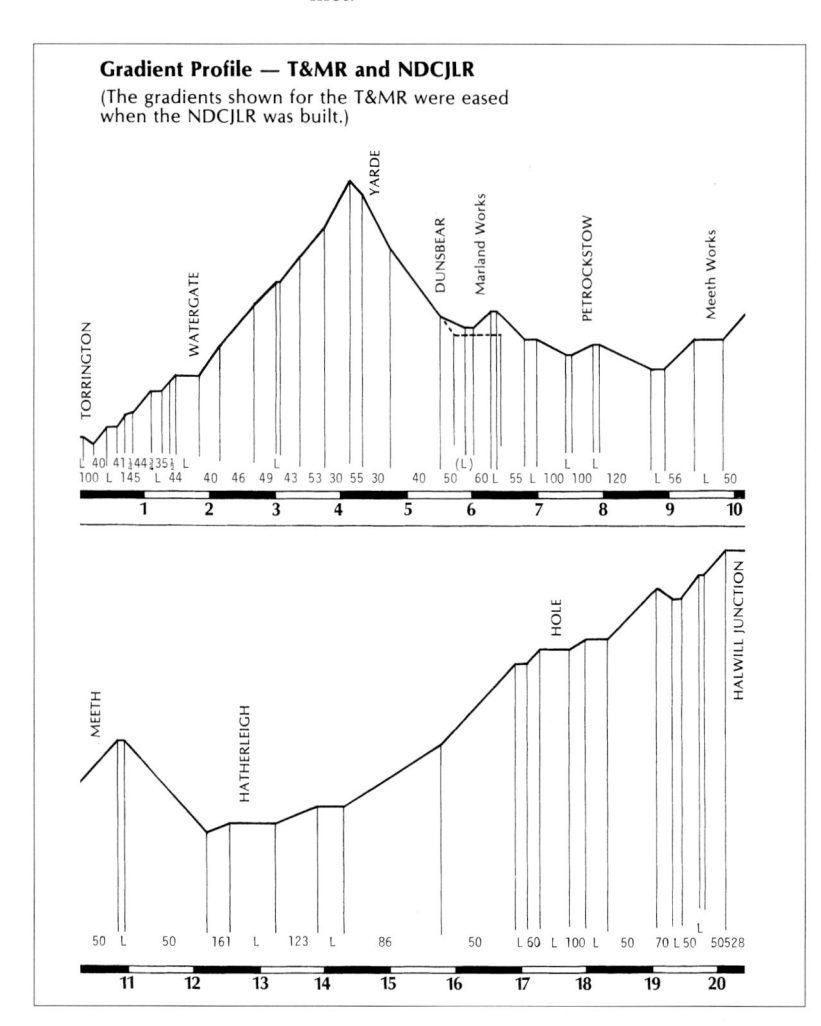

Gradient Profile — T&MR and NDCJLR
(The gradients shown for the T&MR were eased when the NDCJLR was built.)

Major Hall's criticisms were mainly concerning gates, whistle and notice boards and surfacing of platforms, but also with deflection in some of the girder bridges. Additional speed limits were applied to the Torridge Viaduct (10 m.p.h.), the 9 chain reverse curves between Yarde Summit and Bugbear (15 m.p.h.) and at Meeth and Petrockstow crossings (5 m.p.h.).

A speed limit of 25 m.p.h. applied overall, although the Southern cut that to 20 m.p.h. between Torrington and Dunsbear, in view of the curves and gradients, while all engines travelling tender first were limited to 15 m.p.h.. Lower limits of 10 m.p.h. applied to the Torridge Viaduct and the many level crossings. Engines were instructed to whistle continuously for 200 yards at the approach to each crossing. The maximum load of a passenger train was 100 tons, although it is unlikely that this rule was too restrictive. All trains that included goods vehicles had to have a heavy goods brake van at the rear. The Southern headcode for the line was a single disc or headlamp on the right centre of the smokebox. The Marland siding was served by down, Halwill bound, trains. Inwards traffic was left there and outward traffic taken on to Petrockstow to be added to an up train.

Torrington station is 77 feet above sea level and trains faced a steep climb overall to Halwill, at about 600 feet above sea level. The initial four miles or so through the wooded Pencleave Valley to the T&MR summit north of Yarde are at grades of up to 1 in 45, much eased from the 1 in 30 of the narrow-gauge line. The line then drops, at 1 in 42 in places, to Dunsbear where it leaves the former route and, as a newly constructed line, the gradients are much easier. Skirting the lower lying clay moors it is generally downwards until the Little Mere River is crossed

In 1928 LSWR X6 class 4-4-0 waits to leave Hatherleigh with a Torrington bound freight, an unusual working as most trains were mixed.
COLLECTION JOHN NICHOLAS

north of Meeth Works. A brief two-mile climb to a summit just west of Meeth Halt is followed by a drop to cross the River Torridge near Hele Bridge. Then follows an almost continuous climb for the rest of the way to Halwill Junction.

Whilst the Marland brickworks was re-opened in 1925 clay production from both Marland and Meeth failed to reach anything near the anticipated tonnages for very many years. The NDCC workers were carried over the line and Yarde and Watergate Halts were opened for their benefit on 19 July and 20 September 1926 respectively. The first morning train, catering specifically for the clayworkers, left Torrington at 6.25am, just as the narrow-gauge had. Other passenger traffic failed to materialise, which is hardly surprising considering the sparse rural nature of the district. Hatherleigh is the only sizable place and is by road only 7¼ miles (11.7km) from Okehampton, the nearest large centre, whereas by the new rail link it was 20½ miles (33km). Needless to say Hatherleigh people continued travelling by road.

Agricultural depots were established at Hatherleigh and Petrockstow and an abattoir was proposed for Meeth, but not built. As in narrow-gauge days the other sidings were used little. Hatherleigh boasted a station-master and two porter-signalmen, while Petrockstow and Hole had two and one railwaymen respectively. Five permanent way gangs, later three, kept the line in order.

The initial passenger service, worked by the Southern Railway as successor to the LSWR, was three trains each way, later augmented by a couple of short workings to and from Hatherleigh or Petrockstow, to cater for clay workers. By the end of the decade the service had reached its peak of five through trains daily but this was not to last long and in the early thirties the basic pattern that was to continue until withdrawal of the passenger service was established, that is of two through trains each way. Timings were generous, at an hour and twenty minutes or more for the 20½ mile journey, but most trains - all in later years - were scheduled to be mixed and time was needed to pick up freight wagons at stations *en route*.

Traffic figures for the light railway as a whole do not seem to have survived but a Southern record for individual stations has, from 1928 to 1936, and some sort of picture can be gained from the statistics for Petrockstow, Hatherleigh and Hole. Halwill and Torrington have been excluded as no differentiation is shown between the light railway's traffic and the respective main-line and it can be assumed there was little through traffic, the services not catering for it. Passengers using the three stations in 1928 totalled less than 6,000 (70,000 was the 1920 estimate) but dropped to little more than 2,000 in 1936. Petrockstow was the busiest.

Hatherleigh saw most coal and the three stations took 1,500/2,000 tons each year. Obviously the clay works' consumption is not in these figures as their private sidings are excluded from the record. For the same reason there are no figures for clay but we know it did not come up to the 1920 estimate of 85,000 tons a year. Only Petrockstow despatched milk and this was in the years 1929 to 1933 only. It varied considerably and at most was 30,000 gallons. General merchandise accounted for 5/6,000

E1R class 0-6-2T 2695 has arrived at Torrington. The coach is converted from a LSWR steam rail-motor of 1905. May 1935.
H. C. CASSERLEY

The former T&MR trackbed and tunnel are on the right. E1R 2696 leaves Torrington, 1936.
R. W. KIDNER

tons of traffic and Hatherleigh and Petrockstow were busy despatching livestock, the peak being in 1930 when 72 and 204 trucks respectively were sent away.

What was probably the only fatality on the NDCJLR occurred on the morning of 9 September 1932. Whilst shunting at the NDCC siding at Marland the guard, Frederick Rowland, fell under a wagon and was run over. One leg was amputated but he died of his injuries a month later. He had made it clear that no-one was to blame for the accident and a verdict of accidental death was recorded.

The Southern Railway were somewhat short of suitable motive power for their West Country branches and initially used ex-LSWR 4-4-0

Hatherleigh station, soon after the opening, with lower quadrant signals.
JOHN ALSOP COLLECTION

tender engines on the NDCJLR, together with rail-motor carriages which provided both first and third class accommodation. The locomotives were designed by Adams in 1884 for main-line expresses out of Waterloo but as time went by they were relegated to lesser duties and worked their way westward until in 1925 seven were sent to Barnstaple to work the new line. With 6 feet 7 inch diameter driving wheels they can hardly have been ideal for such a steeply graded line and must have been nearly worn out, for when replacements were available they were all scrapped. One had covered well over one million miles in its lifetime.

To remedy the deficiency in motive power a number of E1 class 0-6-0 tank locomotives were rebuilt in 1927/28 as 0-6-2 tanks, designated class E1R, and these were soon to be found on the NDCJLR. The E1s were originally designed by William Stroudley for the London Brighton & South Coast Railway and built between 1874 and 1881. As E1Rs they operated the light railway services for thirty years until, in the late fifties, they were replaced by modern 2-6-2 tanks, designed by H. C. Ivatt in 1946 for the London Midland & Scottish Railway. In due course these were displaced by British Railways' dieselisation programme. Single unit railcars operated the passenger service while North British type 2 diesel-hydraulic locomotives of

Hole station, long enough after opening for the newness to have worn off. Note the lever frame and the lower quadrant signals, later replaced by upper quadrant.
LOCOMOTIVE & GENERAL RAILWAY PHOTOGRAPHS

Petrockstow was very attractively situated at the foot of the hill from the village. In July 1962 Ivatt tank 41297 waits with the 4.37 to Torrington.
R. M. CASSERLEY

1,100 hp took over the freight service until by about 1972 they in turn were displaced by Class 25 diesel-electric locomotives. From 1980 until closure Class 31 diesel electrics ran the freight service to Meeth and Marland. Until dieselisation all trains were scheduled to be mixed.

The NDCJLR continued to exist, of course, although the Southern Railway took full control of their railway, but were solely concerned with administrative details of their company. The Southern were working the line for 75% of the receipts but at no time was the 25% share of the NDCJLR sufficient to pay the 5% interest on the debentures and the Southern always had to make their payment up to £6,500 in accordance with the agreement. In 1934 and 1935, for example, the Southern took £4,919 and £5,056 respectively in traffic receipts but had to pay out the guaranteed £6,500, plus £200 towards NDCJLR office costs, in each year. Both the Devon County Council and the Southern had the right to nominate a director and Lord Clinton was the Southern's nominee from 1926.

H. F. Stephens died on 23 October 1931 and from this time the Southern Railway took over the running of the company; Southern staff providing secretarial and accounting services at Waterloo. In the main the directors met but once a year - at the offices at Exeter, Queen

Yarde Halt in 1967. The products of Exmouth Junction concrete works are prominent.
JOHN ALSOP

84

Activity at Torrington. Ivatt tank 41297 is about to leave for Meeth while the single coach, just arrived from Halwill, on the left, is being added to form the onward connection to Exeter. 30 June 1962. P. W. GRAY

That hub of intermittent life, Halwill Junction. The NDCJLR was confined to an odd bay platform, here occupied by 41283 and its train. From the main westbound platform a train departs for Bude. August 1964. P. W. GRAY

The guard walks to shut the door left by the departing passengers. Yarde Halt in October 1963. Behind the train is the row of cottages built for clay workers and which provided the bulk of passengers here.
M. J. MESSENGER

Street station - but had little to occupy them. In 1936 they complimented the Southern on the line's maintenance and disposed of some small plots of surplus land. With nationalisation in 1948 they accepted the British Transport Commission's offer of £127 for each £100 nominal of debenture stock and 5s for each £100 nominal of ordinary shares.

It did not take long for British Railways to review under-utilised branches and early in 1952 a report set out the position of the NDCJLR. In 1949 just over 28,000 passenger journeys were made, half of those clayworkers to Dunsbear, and over 13,000 parcels carried. Minerals amounted to 36,728 tons, coal and coke 1,280 tons and general merchandise 6,356 tons. Livestock was carried in 482 wagons and Meeth sent 895 churns of milk. The report concluded that if closed to passengers £1,200 in passenger receipts would be lost but only £1,190 in wages and one passenger coach would be saved. Total closure from Hatherleigh to Halwill was considered but 50% of the goods traffic went via Halwill and Hole generated £1,200 of livestock traffic. So the branch survived a little longer.

The following year a lengthy correspondence ensued, between departments of BR, about making economies at Hole. It was proposed to remove the loop and cease as a block station but interdepartmental rivalries kept the argument going. In 1956 F. Cock, the cattle dealer there, said he would transfer his business to road if the loop was removed and two years later it was agreed to keep the loop, as the store had been leased to merchants and some £150 of traffic was expected. In 1955 Cock had sent 87 wagons of livestock generating £1,857 of income, although these figures declined in the following years.

In February 1952 David St John Thomas, writing in the *Western Morning News*, described a visit he had made to the line and made great

In its final years the passenger service was worked by single-unit diesel railcars. One waits here in the bay platform at Halwill Junction while a standard class 4 tank shunts empty coaching stock. September 1964.
M. J. MESSENGER

Table 48

British Railways Summer 1962 timetable.

Miles		am	am SX		am SO		pm SX	pm		Miles		am	am		pm SX	pm SO	
	Halwill ... ... dep	..	1038	..	1052	..	..	6 30	..		Torrington ... ... dep	6 25	8 52	..	4 04	4 40	..
3	Hole	..	1047	...	11 1	..	..	6 39	...	1¾	Watergate Halt.......	6 32	8 59	..	4 7	4 47	...
7¼	Hatherleigh	..	11 5	..	1119	..	..	6 57	...	4½	Yarde Halt..	6 46	9 13	..	4 20	5 1	...
10	Meeth Halt...	..	1116	..	1132	..	..	7 8	...	5½	Dunsbear Halt... ...	6†52	9 18	..	4 25	5 6	...
12¾	Petrockstow	7 55	1126	..	1142	..	4 37	7 18	...	7¾	Petrockstow	..	9 28	..	4 34	5 16	...
14¾	Dunsbear Halt.... ...	8 4	1136	..	1152	..	4 46	7 28	...	10¼	Meeth Halt.........	..	9 38	..	4 44	5 26	...
16	Yarde Halt..	8 10	1141	..	1157	..	4 52	7 34	...	12¾	Hatherleigh	..	9 48	..	4 54	5 36	...
18¾	Watergate Halt.......	8 24	1155	..	1211	..	5 6	7 48	...	17¼	Hole	..	10 8	..	5 13	5 56	...
20¼	Torrington. .. .. arr	8 32	12 2	..	1218	..	5 14	7 56	...	20¼	Halwill .. .. arr	..	1018	..	5 23	6 6	...

SO Saturdays only   **SX** Mondays to Fridays   † Arrival

humour out of the possibility of having a train all to one's self for an afternoon for the sum of 6s.2d, the cost of a return from Torrington to Halwill. Clay workers aside, passenger traffic was sparse but he did note heavy parcels traffic. Apart from train crews, twenty staff - porters, signalmen and permanent-way men - were needed to keep the line operating.

The first withdrawal of facilities came on 2 May 1960 for Watergate and Dunsbear sidings and from 7 September 1964 all goods facilities were withdrawn from the whole line, except for clay traffic. As for passengers BR claimed the line was losing £52,000 a year although the

The 'Exmoor Ranger' special train pulling into Watergate Halt, 27 March 1965.
M. J. MESSENGER

The 'Exmoor Ranger', probably the last through steam train from Halwill, emerges from the Pencleave Valley and is about to cross the Torridge Viaduct. This special train, in which the author was travelling, was hauled by Ivatt tanks 41291 and 41206. It was jointly organised by the Plymouth Railway Circle and the Railway Correspondence & Travel Society on 27 March 1965.
P. W. GRAY

report of the Transport Users Consultative Committee to the Ministry of Transport said the revenue was £1,200 against direct costs of £23,000. There were nine objectors plus Devon County Council at the hearing at Hatherleigh on 2 September and whilst a few people would be personally inconvenienced the objections were very minor. One person used the line once a week. Clay workers were taken home at the end of the day by bus, as there was now no train, and except for Torrington, Yarde and Dunsbear the average number of passengers at each station was in single figures. Closure was a foregone conclusion and the service was withdrawn from 1 March 1965. On 27 March an enthusiasts' special, the steam hauled 'Exmoor Ranger', travelled from Halwill to Torrington and was undoubtedly the last train to travel the full length of the NDCJLR. The section from Meeth to Halwill was then lifted. Petrockstow retained its sidings and signalling until February 1967 when they were removed, although the passing loop was retained.

Clay traffic from the two works continued but in September 1969 BR announced the withdrawal of crane facilities from Fremington Quay, whence much of the clay was shipped. Clay had been exported through Fremington since the 1880s but in 1969 the fifty-year old steam cranes were worn out and BR was unwilling to spend £20,000 replacing them. The clay companies took the opportunity to review their shipping arrangements and the quay at Fremington soon fell silent. The remaining line

The junction for the North Devon Clay Co's siding at Marland, 1979.
M. J. MESSENGER

The Meeth (North Devon) Clay Co siding, from the south, 1979.
M. J. MESSENGER

The last load of clay to leave Meeth waits behind a BR class 31 diesel-electric on 23 August 1982.
RICHARD JOTCHAM

was then worked as a siding from Torrington but later from Barnstaple.

Some 30,000 tons of clay a year travelled by rail, either to Teignmouth or Fowey or to join the Clayliner train to Stoke, but the majority left both works by road. The four-wheeled railway wagon fleet was aging and although some arrangements, including government grants, were made to replace these with modern hopper wagons the NDCJLR would need upgrading to take the new stock. In the event railwaymen's strikes in 1982 precipitated a wholesale switch to road transport and British Rail, with no other traffic for the line, announced total closure from 31 August 1982. The last traffic actually left Meeth on 23 August and Marland on 13 September 1982. Two years later, in June 1984, track-lifting commenced.

With the benefit of hindsight we can see that the North Devon & Cornwall Junction Light Railway was completed too late. The 1920s saw a massive growth in road transport, both public and private, and a commensurate improvement in the roads. The very reasons that in 1920 gave the railway the edge over road were soon removed. This light railway was conceived at a time of great change and was rapidly left behind by rubber-tyred progress. In no way was the expenditure of a quarter of a million pounds on this rural area justified or recouped by the benefits that were gained. Certainly the unemployed of the early 1920s do not seem to have benefited and they, at one time, were the prime concern. Sir Eric Geddes' views on road transport, in the event, were proved to be correct.

CHAPTER NINE
THE MEETH WORKS

The clay deposits in Meeth parish had been known for some time, and were looked at by Henry Holwill in 1895 but, being even more out of the way than the Marland beds, could not be economically worked. However, as the North Devon & Cornwall Junction Light Railway came close to becoming a reality the position changed and no doubt with this in mind Eustace Holwill negotiated for the clay rights at Woolladon and Stockleigh Barton. In 1920 these were transferred to the newly formed Meeth (North Devon) Clay Company Ltd and Eustace was appointed Managing Director.

The first directors were local men - John Tanton Hooper, the owner of Woolladon, and William Balsdon, who took the Chair - but further capital came from the established Cornish and South Devon clay producers. E. J. Hancock and R. R. French, both of St Austell, soon joined the Board and they were later followed by John Lovering and T. S. Donne. All four men were directors of Newton Abbot Clays Ltd and they held shares as nominees for that company. The initial capital was £5,500 in £1 shares but in September 1920 this was increased to £20,000, a much more realistic sum.

Developments were rather slow and Eustace Holwill does not appear to have been the most efficient or competent Managing Director. In June the Directors 'expressed regret that Mr Holwill did not appear to have prepared a definite scheme for the laying out of the works and that things were progressing all too slowly'. They were unanimous that he should resign

Woolladon Pit of the Meeth Works about 1923. The various tools used can be seen and the distinctive water cans for lubrication of the clay balls. On the left is the incline taking the dug clay, sorted as to grade into the appropriate wagon, to the loading stage. On the right, below the wood, can be seen a line used for removing overburden to the tip above.
ECC BALL CLAYS

and, in case he should not, a proposition was left to lay on the table that the company be wound up and reconstituted. Eustace's plea for clemency was rejected as half the company's capital was already spent and he reluctantly resigned in June.

C. J. Channon was appointed Works Manager in August 1920 and progress was rather improved. Pits were opened at Woolladon and Stockleigh, although most work was concentrated on the former as it was closer to the road. The hoisting gear ordered by Holwill arrived in September but it turned out to be nearly useless. A light two-feet gauge line was laid from the pit through Hooper's farmyard to a gantry near the cart track to the road and a vertical boiler and steam winch installed by the pit to haul the side-tipping wagons up the gradient by a cable. A local firm of hauliers, Passmore & Sons, gained the contract to haul the clay to the LSWR at 12s.6d per ton. In the main Okehampton, Sampford Courtenay (where a store was rented) and later Torrington stations were used, although Halwill, North Tawton and Holsworthy were considered as shipping points.

Production commenced in 1921 and the first sales figures available show that 1,377 tons were sold in 1922. The following year 6,729 tons were sold and in 1925 the figure was 9,654 tons; 10,000 becoming the mean for the following few years. More equipment was purchased to handle the increased output; the tramway was extended, a new gantry erected and another portable steam engine bought to replace a Blackstone oil engine. A Petter crude oil engine was also bought to keep the pit dry with a Cornish pump.

Passmores were having difficulty handling the volumes of clay and, despite using five vehicles - Fowler steam waggons and Pierce Arrow lorries - for the traffic, they had to subcontract some. The deteriorating state of the roads, under the additional traffic, was doing the lorries no good and some hauliers would not handle it. To add yet more to their problems Passmores' garage at Okehampton was used as a clay store and the vehicles had to be kept elsewhere. The Rural District Council also complained about the state of the roads, costing the damage at £1,000. They said they would accept a third but the company denied liability and offered £50. Nothing more was heard.

However, the transport problems showed every sign of resolving themselves as the NDCJLR progressed, assisted with £1,200 of Meeth (North Devon) Clay Co.'s money, albeit provided by Newton Abbot Clays Ltd. The line of the standard-gauge railway passed almost a mile from Woolladon but the NDCJLR engineer, Captain Griffiths, surveyed a line connecting the two in 1923. A two-feet gauge tramway was decided on in favour of an aerial ropeway and construction of the earthworks commenced early in 1924, using overburden or 'heading' from the pit.

A Fordson engined petrol locomotive was bought to assist with this work and was evidently more successful than the standard-gauge version the NDCC tried, for a second was bought a year later. The company held the leasehold of Woolladon Moor but east of the Little Mere River a strip of land was leased for £15 a year from James Cobbledick, a director who farmed at Meeth. This was later purchased. By March 1925 the narrow-gauge railway (always referred to in the minutes as 'the tramline') seems to have been completed and a

The standard gauge siding at Meeth, looking north, about 1956.
ECC BALL CLAYS

Clay was tipped direct from two-foot gauge wagons at the main line siding. c1938.
ECC BALL CLAYS

gantry was erected at the standard-gauge siding.

Although the NDCJLR was not yet finished, the route between the Meeth works and Halwill was sufficiently advanced for Colonel Stephens to be able to agree to take clay out by rail and the first truck-loads left in early April. The Colonel charged 3s to 3s.6d for this service but it was provided very much to suit his convenience; he did have a railway to finish building. At first he would only move the clay between noon on Saturday and noon on Sundays but was later prevailed upon to work after 6 pm on weekdays. Even the former was eagerly seized upon for the company had built up a worthwhile number of customers and road transport was becoming more and more unreliable. However, in mid-May the three locomotives of Anderson that the Colonel was using became so perfidious he had to withdraw the evening service. This left the clay company in an unenviable position as they had rearranged the tracks at the pit so as to be convenient for the tramline and could no longer load road wagons there. For the next two months it was with considerable difficulty that any clay was despatched and it must have been a great relief when, on 14 July, the first Southern Railway engine worked out from Halwill Junction to take away seven wagons loaded with Meeth clay.

A siding for the traffic had been part of the agreement with the NDCJLR but the second end had to be added at the company's expense, to make a double-ended siding to permit wagons to be taken on by either up or down trains, according to destination. The NDCJLR opened formally on 27 July 1925 and the Meeth company's transport problems were over, Passmore's services being dispensed with as rapidly as possible.

Andersons, the contractors, had used two-feet gauge railways in the construction of the NDCJLR, as well as three-feet gauge and standard-gauge, and when the railway was finished the opportunity was taken to buy the *Western Lea*, a Hudswell Clarke 0-6-0WT, for £150 as the petrol locomotives were rather expensive to run. Some rails were also bought.

After Eustace Holwill 'resigned', C. J. Channon as Works Manager was in direct charge at the pits but the company was run by R. R. French, as Company Secretary, from St Austell. French worked full-time for the company and appears to have been responsible for all aspects; despatch, sales, accounts and giving Channon his day-to-day instructions. Despite the financial interest the directors of Newton Abbot Clays Ltd played little part in running the business. E. J. Hancock and John Lovering were engrossed in much larger clay works elsewhere and local director William

Meeth Works

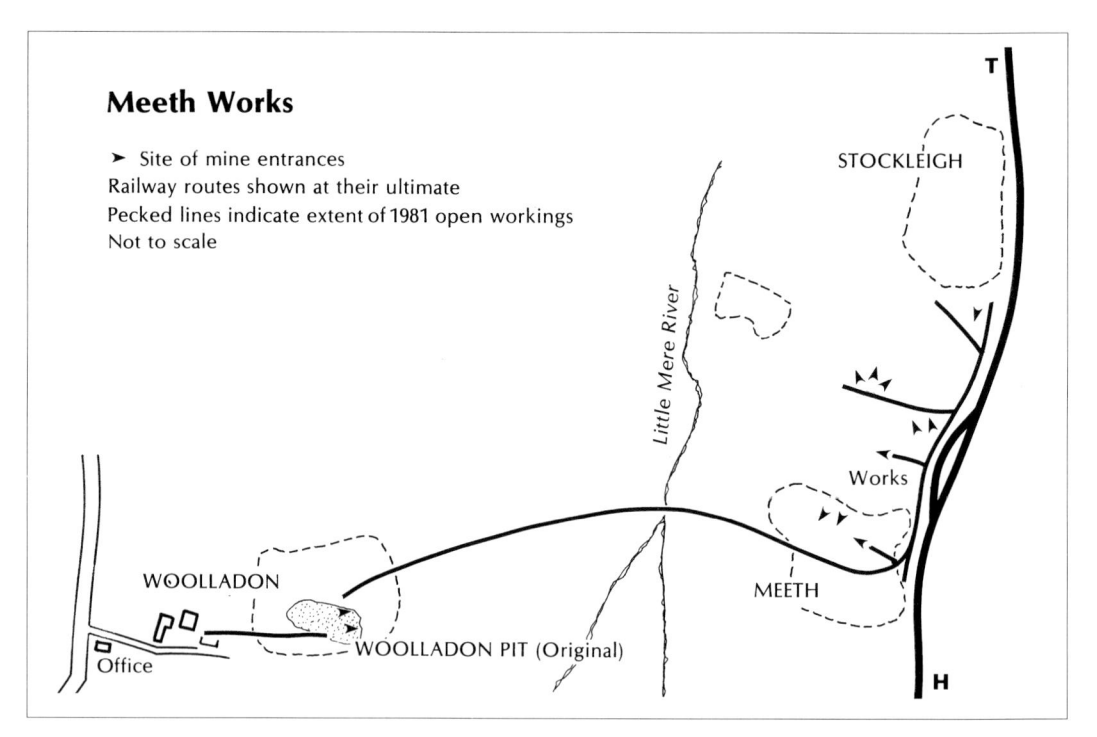

➤ Site of mine entrances
Railway routes shown at their ultimate
Pecked lines indicate extent of 1981 open workings
Not to scale

Balsdon, the Chairman, had a farm and a grocery business in Hatherleigh to attend to. In March 1925 French's involvement was formally recognised when he was appointed Managing Director at a salary of £400 p.a. but he remained at St Austell, some 60 miles away from the works. While this may have been convenient for making contact with purchasers of clay and prospective customers it can hardly have made for close or good management. Employees at this time numbered about 50, three times the 1922 figure. The company controlled the clay rights of some 1,500 acres, having bought more of the Preston-Whyte Estate.

The lengthy coal strike of 1926 handicapped production somewhat, as much because the potteries could not work as because of lack of coal in North Devon, and the works had to resort to a four-day week. Despite this some 10,000 tons were sold. 90% of the clay was sold to, or through, Newton Abbot Clays Ltd and was exported over a wide area of Europe and the USA. Perhaps unfortunately, evidence of the export trade comes from the sources of complaints recorded in the minute books. These mainly related to short weight caused by wetness of the clay, although the absence of a weighbridge could not have helped, and it was

Tipping into Southern Railway wagons at Meeth about 1926, prior to the trans-shipment shed being built.
ECC BALL CLAYS

apparent that a storage shed had to be erected. After deliberation a steel and iron shed costing £275 was purchased.

The method of extracting the balls of clay was the same as at Marland. After exposing the clay by removal of the overburden, the clay was cut in level benches, or 'batches', and the surface marked with a long rake into eight-inch squares. Cutters then dug down with a sharp nine-inch wide spade along and across the rake marks. Water was liberally used to lubricate the tools and the water cans are a prominent feature of photographs. Diggers, a tool with one broad flat blade at right-angles to the handle, were then used to undercut the clay and separate the blocks or balls. They were then 'prodded' across the bench, again lubricated by water, to 'selectors' who directed them into wagons according to grade. The overburden and waste was wheel-barrowed out onto the tip. Some forty or fifty men were employed during the 1920s but less were needed when mining started later. Until Woolladon pit closed, when busy, *Western Lea* would make frequent trips on the tramline taking 16 to 20 tons at a time across to the standard-gauge siding. If the load was heavy it could be split at the loop at the 'bottom' where the line crossed the Little Mere River.

The better clays could be sold direct from the pit but poorer quality clays had to be 'weathered'. The balls were stacked in the open, up to eleven balls high, and left for three or even five years, by which time the weather had washed a good deal of silica out of the clay. This process also seemed to improve the quality of the clay, which could often be sold a grade higher. Wolladon pit provided the best quality clay but it was never as good as at Marland, and Meeth pit was not up to Woolladon standard. Some clay, and more as time went on, was shredded and powdered, although the early processes for doing this were crude in the extreme. Latterly all clay was shredded and weathering became an archaic technique.

The property was continuously surveyed by sinking boreholes and a team of four men was almost constantly engaged on this. Until the advent of modern machinery, boring was done by hand but nevertheless depths of up to 200 feet (60m) were reached. It was a tedious process however.

Despite the improved transport following the opening of the NDCJLR, Newton Abbot Clays Ltd, or their nominees, gave notice at the end of 1926 of their intention to dispose of their shareholdings. It was said that they preferred to concentrate on their own workings in other parts of the West Country but they may have been disillusioned with the slow progress at Meeth. The company was financing itself by an ever increasing overdraft, secured by a mortgage debenture, and profits did appear lacking. The new shareholders, who had a controlling interest in the company, were the Corn and Brain families who had strong interests in the Potteries. The Brain family were directors of F. Brain & Co. Ltd and Coalport China Ltd. The Corns' directorships included the Henry Richards Tile Co. Ltd, - later Richards Tiles Ltd and almost entirely owned by F. R. Corn - Armitage Ware Ltd, Burslem Mills Ltd and Wolstanton Ltd, the last named company operating a colliery. Both families joined the Board and with these interests they were well placed to assist the Devon company.

Mr Corn was well thought of by the men; he introduced one week's holiday with pay. W. H. Brain, as his deputy, took a major part in running the business, partly from his company in Stoke-on-Trent and partly from his home in Torquay, and in March 1929 supplanted French as Managing Director. The office had been moved to the works and J. J. Phillips, French's assistant, became office manager and, later, Company Secretary. In Brain's absence he took much responsibility for the day-to-day running of the works.

More dynamism in the management became apparent and the benefits of outside expertise were made available. One example of this was the employment of a chemist, a Dr Alex Scott, who worked for Brain's pottery, but of far greater impact was the experience the Corns had in collieries. After some investigation it was decided to change to underground extraction of clay and in September 1930 the decision was minuted to work clay beds close to the siding by the 'footrail' method. Despite having driven an underground level at Woolladon in 1927,

The first underground level at Woolladon was driven by C. J. Channon, seen here on the far left at the entrance to the level, in 1927.
ECC BALL CLAYS

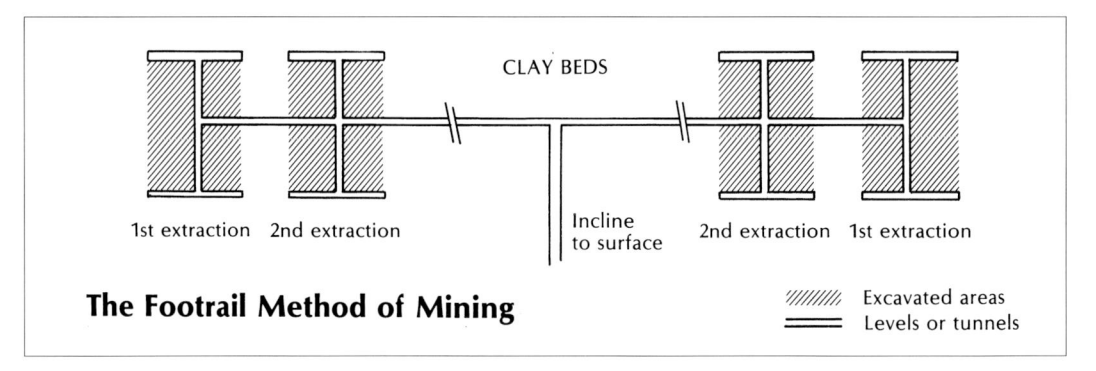

The Footrail Method of Mining

1st extraction 2nd extraction — Incline to surface — 2nd extraction 1st extraction

CLAY BEDS

Excavated areas
Levels or tunnels

Channon was dismissed in 1930 as having insufficient expertise and Mr Stacey, who had worked at Marland, took his place.

The footrail method was to drive a shallow incline from the surface into the clay beds. At the end of the level tunnels were driven off on each side at right-angles through the bed. At their ends similar right angle tunnels were driven parallel to the main incline and at the ends of these the clay was removed for twenty feet on each side, working back to the second tunnel. When all the clay had been removed from this level another was cut sixty feet nearer to and parallel again to the main incline, and the process repeated. Tramways ran down into these levels and wagons were cable hauled along the main drift. At the bottom they were manhandled or moved by winch, and at the surface the small box-like wagons were emptied into those of the surface railway.

Underground working brought the need for compressed air and electricity and steam operated plant was installed, to be replaced when the works was connected to the West Devon Electricity Supply Company's mains in 1934. A reduced workforce also resulted from the change in methods but trading in the early 1930s was very poor and in 1932 W. H. Brain offered to forgo his salary for the year. However, the more economical and efficient system of mining was to prove its worth as time went on.

With the start of production at the new drift mines Woolladon Pit ceased to be worked and equipment was retrieved for use, where possible, elsewhere. *Western Lea* had mainly been used for hauling clay from the pit to the siding and, with the haulage engine at the pit, was laid up in 1931. From that time the tramline was only used for fetching clay stored and stacked for weathering at Woolladon and the one serviceable Fordson sufficed for this. W. H. Brain was succeeded by his son following his death in the mid-thirties and Mr Corn by his nephew, who remained until ECC took over. Lou Stacey, son of the earlier Mr Stacey, became manager having started as fireman on *Western Lea*.

Underground at Meeth. Steel arches are in use here. ECC BALL CLAYS

THE MEETH WORKS

Ruston diesel 237897 stands out of use on the two-foot gauge. May 1968.
M. J. MESSENGER

The soft ground at Meeth necessitated standard gauge sleepers to spread the weight of narrow gauge trains. May 1968.
M. J. MESSENGER

One of the Ruston diesels propelling wagons to the loading point alongside the NDCJLR. About 1965. BALL CLAY HERITAGE SOCIETY

The Second World War cut off overseas markets and clay was stockpiled in anticipation of peace. New mines were opened after the War, the original No 1 mine lasting until 1960, and Woolladon Pit was reopened. In 1965 English China Clays Limited, the St Austell company who dominated the world china clay market, bought the share capital and in 1967 the assets were transferred to another ECC subsidiary, Hexter & Budge Ltd, who operated the group's ball clay pits in South Devon. At the same time the Meeth (North Devon) Clay Company Limited had its name changed to Meeth Ball Clays (ECC) Limited, and in 1979, assetless, was wound up. Hexter & Budge Limited became ECC Ball Clays Limited in 1970.

The wheel had turned a full circle, for the founding directors of ECC were none other than those early directors of the Meeth (North Devon) Clay Co. Ltd., John Lovering, E. J. Hancock and T. S. Donne. As in the earlier change in management, changes in techniques followed and, here too, the wheel had come a full circle, for a reversion to open pit working followed. As was soon to happen at Marland, the railway was displaced by dumper trucks and all the equipment was scrapped in 1970. By the mid-seventies all production was from pits, which gave greater access to the clay, at Meeth and Woolladon and in 1976 a new pit was opened at Stockleigh. Woolladon Pit production has been run down but during the 1970s production gradually climbed from about 40,000 tons a year to 60,000 tons. Half this was exported, via Bideford, Teignmouth and Fowey, and until the rail link closed in 1982, one-third was despatched by rail to Stoke-on-Trent. Following 1982 all clay left Meeth by road.

In 1999 the ECC Group was taken over by Imerys, a French company, but production continued at the same levels, about 60,000 tons a year. However, the poorer quality clay of Meeth became its downfall as better grades could be obtained by the company from South Devon and Dorset. Production finally ceased in December 2004 and the works closed. For the time being the site is being used by WBB Minerals for storage but in due course the land will be restored.

CHAPTER TEN
LOCOMOTIVES AND ROLLING STOCK OF MEETH

In the early 1920s a light railway was the only way to move any useful quantity of material in a quarry or pit and the purchase of rails and equipment was high on Eustace Holwill's priorities. Rails were bought from the Monmouth & South Wales Colliery Owners Pitwood Association and a locomotive too was ordered from them. The Association operated a shortlived twenty-inch gauge line at an as yet unknown forestry site in the Torrington area to meet the wartime and postwar shortage of timber pit-props. They possessed a Motor Rail 'Simplex' petrol locomotive and presumably it is this that Eustace Holwill ordered, but the order was cancelled following his 'resignation'. The works then had no need of a locomotive as the skip wagons were hauled up an incline out of the pit straight on to a tipping dock where the load was transferred to lorries or storage.

FORDSON TRACTORS
When the 'tramline' was constructed across the valley to the NDCJLR a locomotive became necessary because a run of a mile was involved. A Fordson petrol/paraffin locomotive was bought, possibly at Colonel Stephens' suggestion, for he had suggested a standard gauge locomotive of the same manufacture to the North Devon Clay Co. Strictly speaking it was not a locomotive as such that was bought but a conversion kit. The local Ford dealers, T. Day & Sons Ltd of Okehampton, ordered from Muir-Hill of Trafford Park, Manchester, a chassis unit on to which they mounted a 20 hp engine and transmission unit from a Fordson tractor. The whole thing weighed about 4 tons, and was carried on and driven through four wheels 20 inches diameter and of 38 inches wheelbase. The approximate dimensions were: overall length 9 feet 9 inches, overall width 4 feet 6 inches and height from rail, including the canopy, 7 feet 6 inches. Although normal running was on paraffin, for economy, a small petrol tank was provided for ease of starting, the engine being switched over to paraffin fuel when warm. With an additional gearbox to give a range of speeds in reverse a capable small locomotive was obtained for £300.

The first was bought in March 1924 and a second, possibly of improved design for it cost a little more, arrived twelve months later. The tractors had the advantage that they could be switched off when not needed but this may have been better in theory than in practice for such petrol/paraffin engines could be particularly difficult to start. The company was finding their's expensive to run and at the sale of Andersons' plant bought a steam engine, perhaps also thinking of the heavier loads they expected to be carrying across the moor.

The tractors probably saw little further use until 1931, when *Western Lea* was laid up, and were not in good condition. The older was

This Muir-Hill publicity leaflet describes the type of locomotive used at Meeth and the illustration is similar to the second one supplied there.
AUTHOR'S COLLECTION

WESTERN LEA after it had moved on from Meeth to the Standard Brick Co., Redhill.
B. D. STOYEL

Ruston 48DL 260118 of 1948 stands locked up for the weekend at Meeth, June 1967. MICHAEL BISHOP

cannibalised to keep the other going. Following the arrival of the Ruston & Hornsby diesels after the Second World War the frame of one was converted to a shelter for an electric winch at one of the mine entrances. Eventually one set of frames and an engine went away for preservation, while the rest of the remains were scrapped.

Western Lea

Like all contractors of the time Andersons made heavy use of steam engines in the construction of the NDCJLR, utilising railways of standard, three-feet and two-feet gauges, depending on the needs of the terrain.

The only steam locomotive on the last named gauge was the *Western Lea*. This was a six-coupled well-tank built by Hudswell Clarke & Co. Ltd in 1918 to a standard design developed for the War Office in 1914. Most were of 60cm gauge but 1314 was one of the few built to two-feet and part of an uncompleted order for 20 locomotives intended for the Italian front, but the cessation of hostilities caused it to be delivered to Kidbrooke Aerodrome in London. From here it was sold to Nott Brodie & Co. Ltd who used it for construction of the Bristol to Avonmouth 'Portway Road', before selling it to Andersons.

The Meeth company bought it from Andersons' Receiver, following the auction sale in September 1925, at a cost of £150. *Western Lea* was a robust and practical locomotive, designed for rough work. It had outside Walschaert valve gear and a wheelbase of 50 inches. Overall length was 15 feet and the weight in working order 7⅓ tons. It served Meeth well but had only a short working life there as on the closure of Woolladon Pit it became redundant. It was

Conventional side-tip wagons were used on the surface line at Meeth but were modified with wooden bodies to prevent the clay being stained. May 1968.
M. J. MESSENGER

laid up in 1931 and sold late in 1933 for £50 to the Mansfield Standard Sand Co. Ltd.

From Meeth the locomotive appears to have gone to Peckett's works in Bristol for overhaul before being delivered to the Standard Brick & Sand Co. Ltd at Redhill. From here it was disposed of in 1936 but whether for work elsewhere or scrap is not known.

Ruston & Hornsby diesels
The Fordson tractors managed the little traffic that needed hauling across from Woolladon until after the Second World War when increased production and the reopening of Woolladon Pit called for better motive power, even if only on the tracks connecting the mines with the storage sheds and the main-line siding. Two Ruston & Hornsby four-wheel diesel locomotives of type 30DL were bought in 1945 and 1948. These sturdy machines weighed about four tons and were of 30 hp. The older locomotive fell out of use by the mid 1960s but the newer one was working until the late sixties. Both were sold for scrap in August 1970.

Rolling Stock
The standard wagon used was the ubiquitous two-ton side-tipping V-skip but these varied from the normal design by having wooden sides and ends to the skips. These were introduced from November 1922 and were to prevent the clay becoming rust stained. Most were supplied by Robert Hudson Ltd, of Leeds, and quite how many there were, or were serviceable, is not known but fifty or sixty is indicated. No doubt the frames of some were modified for other purposes, such as flat wagons, but all were scrapped in 1970.

See Appendix 3 for details of the locomotives.

Small four wheel tub wagons were used at Meeth to bring clay up to surface. May 1968.
M. J. MESSENGER

CHAPTER ELEVEN
THE TWENTY-FIRST CENTURY

The clay industry has changed enormously in recent decades, particularly since the first edition of this book.

ECC Ball Clays, along with its parent company, has become part of Imerys plc, a multinational organisation. Meeth works has now closed and its story concluded. Marland continues to expand although production methods are now very efficient using a minimal workforce and modern equipment. WBB, successors to the North Devon Clay Company, has been acquired by SCR - Sibelco, a Belgian company.

The route of the North Devon & Cornwall Junction Light Railway has been preserved for a considerable distance and, from Torrington to Meeth Halt, forms part of the Tarka Trail. The route can now be easily explored walking or cycling.

The Torridge Viaduct survives to take the Trail across the river and the stone built platforms of the halts at Watergate, Yarde, Dunsbear and Meeth can all be seen. Meeth still has its waiting hut. Of the stations, Petrockstow has lost its station building but some goods sheds survive as part of a Council depot in the former goods yard. Hatherleigh and Hole are now private houses. At the two ends of the line Torrington station is very intact - the station building is now an attractive pub with a strong railway theme - but Halwill Junction has all but disappeared without trace. With a touch of possibly unintentional irony a small housing development on the site is named Beeching Close.

Remains of Fell's Torrington & Marland Railway do survive but are harder to find. At Torrington the tunnel under the road can be seen, blocked up, and a solitary brick stump of a viaduct pier is on the south bank of the river. For many years piers remained in the river but were removed to prevent debris building up on them in times of flood.

Barley Hayes is on of the few underbridges on the NDCJLR and is built of Marland bricks. It was the site of a timber viaduct in T&MR days and in its abutments can be detected the remains of part of the earlier structure.

The route and remains of the T&MR were almost totally obliterated in the building of the NDCJLR but occasional clues can be gained where the boundary fence is a little wider than expected, the standard gauge line having taken a slightly easier course. At Summit, just north of Yarde, the NDCJLR is at a lower level and the old T&MR loop is above the cutting, on the west side, but now completely overgrown.

Rather more is visible south of Dunsbear where the two railway routes diverge and a section of the T&MR remains untouched. For the first few yards the route has become part of the field but a low embankment is soon apparent. What the 1885 Ordnance Survey describes as a viaduct is now a small simple arched occupation bridge, built of both Marland and engineering bricks, and this may be later than the railway. Approaching the works the embankment increases in height and may have replaced an earlier timber viaduct approaching and crossing the River Mere. There was later a girder bridge here and some remains are still in place but look somewhat unsafe. Within the works most buildings are large modern structures to suit present day needs but the office remains in use and the former weighbridge building survives, as do parts of the trans-shipment building and standard gauge engine shed. Parts of the old carpenters shops can be seen and standard gauge rails still run through undergrowth.

Ball clay will continue to be extracted for as long as the deposits are there and as long as there is a demand. The new techniques of extraction, however, together with changing public attitudes towards the environment, have resulted in greater concern being shown by the clay companies to the impact of their workings on the landscape. This, combined with the knowledge that the clay is not inexhaustible, has resulted in much more care and thought than ever before being given to the future.

APPENDIX ONE
TORRINGTON & MARLAND RAILWAY
THE ENGINEER'S SPECIFICATION, PRICES AND QUANTITIES

The following pages are a transcript of the original hand-written specification, schedule of prices and bill of quantities provided by J. B. Fell and his son, G. N. Fell, in 1879. They provide a rare insight into the engineer's and contractor's view of a relatively minor contract. The spelling, grammar and punctuation have been retained, except that 'breadth' has been substituted for 'breath', which is used consistently in error.

TORRINGTON & MARLAND RAILWAY
GENERAL SPECIFICATION

This Railway commences at the Torrington Station on the London and South Western Railway and terminates at the Marland Clay and Brick Works. The length of the line is 6 miles 2 furlongs and the gauge is 3 feet.

The Railway will be made on Mr J B Fell's Improved System for the construction of Light Railways which consists in the formation of the line principally upon timber viaducts in place of earthworks and masonry for which they are substituted on the parts of the line where the Ballast and permanent way cannot be laid on the surface or where the cuttings and embankments would if made exceed a depth of about 3 feet.

The Plan of the Railway is shewn on Contract Drawing No 1. The section is shewn on drawing No 2, the cuttings being coloured green, the embankments red and the viaducts and bridges yellow.

EARTHWORKS

Cross sections of the Railway in cutting and embankments are shown in drawing No 3. When in cutting the width at formation level is ten feet exclusive of the side ditches or gutters of one foot each. The width of the embankments at formation level is ten feet.

The slopes of both cuttings and embankments are to be 1 to 1 or 1½ to 1 as may be required, excepting in rock when they will be ¼ or ½ to 1. The earth from the cuttings will be put into the embankments excepting in the case of the cutting at the Torrington Station where it may be taken by the South Western Company or otherwise disposed of so that no lead need be taken into account for that cutting. The slopes on both cuttings and embankments must be soiled with a depth of three inches of loam or vegetable earth and sown with grass seeds.

CULVERTS

The culverts will be made of earthenware drain pipes in all cases where pipes of not more than 16 inches diameter will be sufficient and for culverts of a larger size there will be open water courses over which the rails will be laid upon a suitable length of the timber viaduct structure.

VIADUCTS AND BRIDGES

The viaducts when from 3 to 15 feet in height will be made upon the designs shewn in drawings Nos 4 and 5 and 5a and when from 15 to 30 feet in height they will be made on the designs shewn in drawings Nos 6, 7 & 8.

The bridge over the river Torridge and the viaduct adjoining it where the same exceeds 35 feet in height will be made on the design shewn in drawings Nos 9 and 10.

The form of girder shown in drawing No 5 being a lattice girder combined with longitudinal supporting struts is to be used throughout the line excepting in special cases when other forms may be ordered by the Company's Engineer.

The supports shown in drawing No 5a are to be used for every alternate length of structure where the Railway is on a straight line or on curves of more than ten chains radius. Where the curves are ten chains radius and under the No 5a form of support is to be used exclusively and where the No 5a form of support is not required then the support shown in No 4 is to be used. Lateral stays are in like manner to be provided for the supports shown in drawings Nos 8 and 10. The length of the foundations of the Torridge Bridge are also to be increased from 16 to 18 feet and the lateral stays carried up to the level of the longitudinal struts.

The foundations of the Bridge over the river Torridge are shown in Drawings Nos 9, 10 and 10a. They are formed of 10 Baltic red pine piles of 10 inches square so each foundation or pier of the Bridge of which there are two to be formed in the bed of the river Torridge. The other supports of the Bridge being on solid ground on the Banks on either side of the River. The piles are to be driven to a depth of six feet in the bed of the river provided there is no rock or boulders to prevent their being driven to that depth. In the event of the piles being driven to a less depth than four feet the foundations must be protected by rubble stones being laid round them to a depth of three feet where in contact with the piers and laid to a slope of 1 to 1 on the river side of the foundations. The heads of the piles are to be held together laterally by cross ties as shown in drawing No 10 and 3 inch planking is to be spiked or otherwise firmly secured on to the piles as shown in the drawings for a height of 6 or 7 feet above the level of the river.

The foundations or piers of the Bridge are to be placed at right angles to the direction of the line as it crosses the river. The upright supports of the piers above the level of the foundations which are 6 inches and 8 inches square resptly are to be halved and bolted on to the foundation piles. The upright supports [of the piers above the level of the foundations which are 6 inches and] 8 inches square [resptly] are to be placed vertically under the carrying rails & girders and those 6 inches square are to be placed under the handrailing. The total width of the piers being 8 feet in addition to which lateral stays will be fixed from the bottom of the longitudinal struts to the foundations in order to give increased lateral stability to the bridge.

An overbridge at the Turnpike Road at the Torrington Station is to be provided, 60 feet in length 9 feet in width and 10 feet 6 inches in height from the level of the rails with a semicircular arch. The arch is to be built of brickwork and the side and wing walls of rubble masonry. The quantity of Brickwork in the Bridge will be about 40 cubic yards and the rubble masonry about 160 cubic yards.

All viaducts are to be made of Baltic red pine timber and deals of good quality and generally free from shakes and dead knots. The girders and supports are to be fished framed and bolted together in a workmanlike manner. The supports where not more than 15 feet in height are to be sunk 18 inches into the ground and the earth firmly punned in round them. Where the supports are to be 15 to 30 feet in height they will be sunk 2 feet into the ground and when 30 to 40 feet in height from 2 feet to 3 feet into the ground or to such other depth in either case as the Engineer may deem necessary.

The bolts washers and plates are to be made of the best Staffordshire or an equally good quality of iron tapped and screwed with the Whitworth thread.

The wooden lattice girders are when so required by the Engineer to have the lattice bars recessed and framed together at the intersections of each bar the recess being cut to a depth of from half-an-inch to 1 inch. The four longitudinal pieces in each girder when these are 15 feet or 18 feet in length will be 5 inches in breadth and 2 or $2\frac{1}{2}$ in thickness or 4 inches in breadth and 3 inches in thickness. The lattice bars will be $3\frac{1}{2}$ inches in breadth and $2\frac{1}{2}$ in thickness or 4 inches by 2 inches or 3 inches in breadth by 3 inches in thickness.

The girders are to be put together and fastened to the supports with $\frac{5}{8}$ and $\frac{3}{4}$ inch bolts with square heads and nuts. The washers are to be $2\frac{1}{2}$ inches square $\frac{3}{16}$ inch thick.

The fish plates are to be 14 inches long 3 inches wide and $\frac{1}{4}$ inch thick. In erecting the timber viaducts care must be taken that the supports are set vertically and the girders true to the gradients of the Railway. The angles or spaces between them and the corbels on the supports are to be filled up when necessary with wedged shaped pieces of wood so as to give the girders a solid bearing upon the whole length of the corbels. Upon the curves the girders will form a series of short straight lines placed at slight angles to one another. The fish plates must be bent to these angles and the spaces between the girders and the supports wherever it is possible to do so must be filled up as before described.

The cross ties of the structure must be spiked down to the girders in such a manner as not to split the longitudinals and the rails will be laid on the cross ties in the usual way the joints will be secured with fang bolts and $3\frac{1}{2}$ inch dog nails will be used for the intermediate fastenings of which there will be two for each rail to each sleeper or cross tie.

The supports, where not more than 15 feet in height are to be sunk 18 inches into the ground and the earth firmly punned in round them. When the supports are 15 to 30 feet in height they will be sunk 2 feet into the ground and when 30 to 40 feet in height from 2 feet to 3 feet into the ground or to such other depth in either case as the Engineer may deem necessary and both the girders and the supports are to be made of a kind of Baltic Timber sufficiently strong to carry a sixwheel engine of six tons weight the axles being 5 feet apart. The axles of the waggons being placed at the same distances and carrying the same loads as the engine axles.

The dimensions of the different parts of the viaduct work and of the Bridge over the river Torridge are shewn in the drawings excepting the thickness of the lattice bars or struts of the Bridge which is 4 inches. The breadth of these is shewn being 8 inches. The whole of the timber work is to be coated with a mixture of Gas Tar and Pitch and the mixture to be laid on while hot.

PERMANENT WAY

The rails are to be of the Vignolles or Bridge form and will be provided by the Marland Company. The sleepers are to be of oak cut square and free from sap 6 feet long, 7 inches broad and $3\frac{1}{2}$ inches thick or 6.0 x 8 x 4 if of Baltic pine timber.

The points of the rails are to be fished with plates and bolts of suitable size and to be securely fastened with 3 and 4 inch dog-nails to the sleepers which are to be laid 2 feet 6 inches aprt from centre to centre.

The bottom ballast is to be formed of broken stone loose gravel or quarry rubbish and to be 1 foot in depth under the sleepers. The top ballast is to be sand or gravel taken from the cuttings or the beds of rivers on or near the line. Ballast drains must be made where necessary. A plan and cross section of the permanent way and Ballast is given in drawing No 3. On curves the outside rail must have given to it a superelevation such as may be required by the radius of the curve and as directed by the Engineer.

STATIONS SIDINGS &C
A sum of £500 is to be included in the tender for stations, sidings, points and crossings, level crossings, signals, engine shed, water tanks, turntables, for 2 Gates 10 feet long each and two chains for each level crossing of which there will be five and 3,520 lineal yards of 3 rail fencing posts to be 5" x 3" or 4 x 4 rails 3" x 1¼" of larch or red pine timber will be required.

ROYALTIES
All royalties that may become chargeable for the use of the patents or patent rights in the construction of the Railway Rolling Stock and appurtenances are to be paid by the Contractor.

OCCUPATION OF LAND
All the necessary land roads rights and powers for the execution of the works of the railway whether for permanent or temporary occupation or for ballast and such as may be required for the execution and completion of this Contract are to be furnished by the Company free of charge to the Contractors.

SETTING OUT OF LINE
The Company's Engineer will set out the Line and furnish the Contractor with the necessary detailed drawings and directions as the works proceed. The chain men labourers and materials required in setting out the line will be provided by the Contractors.

MATERIALS
All the materials supplied both as regards their dimensions kind and quality and also the work executed shall be to the satisfaction and subject to the approval of the Company's Engineer who shall have the power of rejecting any portion of the materials or of the work either before or after it has been employed upon the Railway and he may order such defective portions of the work to be renewed and replaced at the expense of the contractor.

COMMENCEMENT AND COMPLETION OF WORKS
The works are to be commenced within one month of the date of the contract and are to be completed within seven months from the time of their commencement cases of 'force majeur' excepted.

MAINTENANCE
The Contractor will keep the Railway and Works comprised in the Contract in good and substantial repair for the period of six calendar months from the date when the works shall have been completed and shall deliver up the said works and railways to the Company cases of 'force majeur' excepted in good and substantial repair and condition.

PAYMENT
The payment for the works executed and for the materials delivered on the ground on or near the line of Railway are to be made by the Company on the Engineer's certificates monthly and within a week of the end of each calendar month.

The monthly payments on account are to be made at the rate of 90 per cent of the Schedule of Prices annexed and the remaining 10 per cent is to be paid one half on the completion of the works of the contract and the other half at the expiration of the six months included in the term of maintenance.

The Contractor shall have the use of the permanent way material and Rolling Stock free of charge and he must deliver up the same to the Company at the completion of the contract in good condition allowing for ordinary wear and tare [sic].

John B Fell CE

Richd Jameson
Secretary Greenodd Railway & General Contracting Company Limited

SCHEDULE OF PRICES
to regulate the monthly payments on account of materials and works executed

DESCRIPTION OF MATERIALS WORKS &c	QUANTITY	PRICE
Sleepers Oak 6'0" x 7" x 3½" Red Pine 6'0" x 8" x 4"	each	2s
Bolt and Plates for Viaducts and bridges fish plate and fang bolts and dog nails	per ton	£15
Ballast delivered along the line	per cubic yard	2s 6d
Permanent way complete (without rails) with sleepers fastenings and Ballast	per linear yard	7s
Baltic red pine and other timber and deals planks scaffolding &c	per cubic foot	2s
Bolts washers and fishplates for viaduct work	per ton	£17
Lattice girders complete 15 feet long	each	£1 13s
Ditto Ditto 18 ditto	each	£2 2s
Viaduct supports complete drawings Nos 4 and 5 & 5a	per ft of height	4s
Ditto Ditto Nos 7 and 8	ditto	6s
Works executed in Bridge over the Torridge and Viaduct Drawings Nos 9 and 10	per cubic ft	3s 10d
Forming line earthwork in cuttings & embankments not exceeding 6 feet in depth	per lineal yard	5s
Ditto exceeding 6 feet in depth	per cubic yd	1s 4d
Rubble masonry in Bridges &c	per cubic yard	17s 6d
Brick work in arches	ditto	30s

John B Fell CE
Richard Jameson
Secretary &c

TORRINGTON AND MARLAND RAILWAY
QUANTITIES

Earthworks
    Light bank and cutting up to 3 feet in depth   8,500 cu yds
    Bank and cutting exceeding 3ft in depth 21,000 cu yds   29,500 cu yds
Masonry   150 cu yds
Permanent way   Tons cwts qr
    Rails 30 lbs pr lin yd   295 .0 .0
    Fish plates & bolts   25 .0 .0
    Dog nails & spikes   7 .0 .0
    Fang bolts   6 .5 .0
    Sleepers -   6'0" x 8" x 4" - 8976
        do   4'6" x 7" x 3" - 4224   13,200
Foot plank & guard rail in Viaducts - Timber   2,000 cu ft
Ballast   7,500 cu yds
Viaducts - Timber work   Cu ft
    70 chains averaging   5ft in height   6,407
    49   10ft   5,703
    22   15ft   3,056
    11   20ft   1,656
    2   25ft   461
    1   30ft   228
    4   35ft   1,212
    Bridge over the River Torridge   2,783

        Total no of cu feet   21,566

Iron work   Tons cwts qrs
    Bolts   25 .6 .2
    Plates & washers   10 .8 .0
    Spikes   2 .0 .0

     37 .14 .2

APPENDIX ONE

			m	f	chs
Castings			0. 18 .0		
Shoes for foundation piles			0 .7 .1		
Viaducts			m	f	chs
Average height	5 feet length			7	0
	10 ft			4	9
	15 ft			2	2
	20 ft			1	1
	25 ft				2
	30 ft				1
	35 ft				4
Bridge over the River Torridge					3
Total length of Viaduct			2	0	2
Cutting	under 3 ft in depth		1	0	8
do	over 3ft			6	3
Bank formed out of cuttings			1	4	2
Surface line				6	5
Total length of Railway			6	2	0

Stations
    Sidings, points & crossings, level crossings, signals,
    engine shed, water tanks, turntables, etc
    as per specification   £750

Rolling stock
    1 Locomotive engine £850
    20 wagons @ £45 each £900

Geo N Fell CE, 9 Dec 1879

APPENDIX TWO
OPERATING COSTS OF THE TORRINGTON & MARLAND RAILWAY

The surviving papers of the North Devon Clay Co. Ltd, include two accounts of the cost of running the three-feet gauge line. Both are undated but appear to have been prepared to meet the possibility of a standard gauge replacement. The first would seem to be from the late 1890s, and a result of the Torrington & Okehampton Railway proposals, while the second was from the time of the Great War, with the North Devon & Cornwall Junction Light Railway in mind. Both, of course, are in pre-decimal currency.

A. Driver & stoker — £2.15s.0d per week
Six packers — £5. 0s.0d per week
Coal and oil — £3.10s.0d per week
Smith & mate — £1.0s.0d per week
Fitter — £1.0s.0d per week
Carpenter — <u>15s.0d per week</u>
£14. 0s.0d per week
= £728 per annum

Material for Permanent Way — £75 per annum
Material for Rolling Stock — £100 per annum
Rent, Rates & Taxes — £60 per annum
Sundry — <u>£137</u> per annum
Cost of working line — £1,000 per annum
(*sic* - the error is in the original)

Less receipts from public traffic — <u>£300</u> per annum
£700
Rent — <u>£600</u>
Total Cost — £1,300

Notes: The larger figure for rent is that due to the Misses Wren under the lease. Sundry may include the cost of trans-shipment at Torrington.

B. Cost of Working Marland Line (Normal Times)

	per week	per annum
Wages Fitters & Smiths Shops	£13.18s.4d	
for Railway say one half per week	£6.1 9s.2d	
Carpenter, one full time	£3.7s.3d	
2 Engine Drivers & Stokers	£11 .6s.5d	
Packers	£22.2s.2d	
Berry Moor (sic)	£2.0s.0d	
Transfer Men	<u>£21.0s.0d</u>	
	£66.15s.0	£3,471
Fitter & Smiths Shops, Oil & Materials		104
Coal		550
Oil & Waste		100
Engineers' a/cs		600
Firebox renewals		150
Timber for repair of Viaducts		200
Timber for Sleepers		200
Rails (renewals)		300
Rents		33
Rates		60
		£5768
Less Receipts for Public Traffic		<u>300</u>
		£5468

'This amount would carry 30,000 tons, equalling 3/6 per ton. Only a small reduction can be effected if one half the quantity is carried. We assume that if 15,000 tons only are carried per annum the cost per ton would be 6/- at least. If the new railway is made we should still have to reckon for transfer at Works instead of Station say £10 per week. After paying for Workmen's tickets and carriage of clay etc, on new line we should save £2,000 to £3,000 per annum and more in proportion if output were reduced.'

APPENDIX THREE
LOCOMOTIVES OF MARLAND AND MEETH

North Devon Clay Company Ltd
3 feet gauge

Name	Type	Maker	Maker's No	Year Built	Cylinders (inches)	Driving Wheel	Wheel Base	Origin	Disposed
Mary	0-6-0ST	Black Hawthorn	576	1880	7½ x 10	20"	9 feet	New	Scr c1925
Tudor	0-4-0IST	Bagnall	265	1879	6 x 9	18"		Hired	by 1888
Marland	0-6-0T	Bagnall	566	1883	7½ x 10	20"	9 feet	New	Scr c1925
Peter	0-4-0T	Lewin		1877	5¾ x 9 ?	21"	3 feet	Bought c1884	Scr by 1923
Coffeepot	0-4-0VB	Head Wrightson ?		1870s				Bought c1884	Scr about 1908
Avonside	0-6-0ST	Avonside	1428	1901	7 x 10	33"	9 feet	New	Scr c1925
Jersey I	0-4-0	Fletcher Jennings	129	1873	9 x 16	33"		Bought 1908	Scr 1949
Jersey II	0-4-0	Fletcher Jennings	139	1874	9 x 16	33"		Bought 1908	Scr 1952
Merton	0-4-0	Fletcher Jennings	150	1875	9 x 16	33"		Bought 1908	Scr 1949
Forward	4wDM	Fowler	3900012	1927	40hp			New	Scr 1970
Advance	4wDM	Fowler	3930037	1949	40hp			New	Scr 1970
Efficiency	4wDM	Fowler	3930048	1951	40hp			New	Sold 1974
-	4wDM	Ruston & Hornsby	435398	1959	48hp			New	Sold 1972
Efficiency	4wDM	Ruston & Hornsby	446207	1961	48hp			New	Scr 1971
-	4wDM	Ruston & Hornsby	435393	1959	48hp			Bought 1965	Scr 1969
-	4wDH	Ruston & Hornsby	518187	1965	48hp			New	Scr 1971

Standard Gauge

Name	Type	Maker	Maker's No	Year Built	Cylinders (inches)	Driving Wheel	Wheel Base	Origin	Disposed
-	4wPM	Muir-Hill	A137	1926	25hp	40"		New	Returned 1926
No 79	0-6-0ST	Manning Wardle	1049	1888	12 dia			Bought 1925	Scr c1946
Mersey	0-4-0ST	Black Hawthorn	1059	1892	12 dia			Bought 1925	Scr 1950
Progress	0-4-0DM later DH	Fowler	4000001	1945	60hp			New	Sold 1988
Peter	0-4-0DM	Fowler	22928	1940				Bought 1950	Sold 1988
-	4wDM	Ruston & Hornsby	443642	1960	48hp			Bought 1975	Sold 1988

Although some sources give numbers for the locomotives they did not carry running numbers and those quoted are boiler numbers for insurance purposes. These appear to have varied from time to time and are inconsistent.

Meeth (North Devon) Clay Company Ltd
2 feet gauge

Name	Type	Maker	Maker's No	Year Built	Cylinders (inches)	Driving Wheel	Wheel Base	Origin	Disposed
-	4wPM	Muir-Hill	-	1924	20hp	20 inches	38 inch	New	Scr
-	4wPM	Muir-Hill	A110	1925	20hp	20 inches	38 inch	New	Sold 1970
Western Lea	0-4-0WT	Hudswell Clarke	1314	1918	6½ x 12	23 inches	50 inch	Bought 1925	Sold 1933
No 1	4wDM	Ruston & Hornsby	237897	1945	30hp			New	Sold for scrap 1970
-	4wDM	Ruston & Hornsby	260118	1948	30hp			New	Sold for scrap 1970

APPENDIX FOUR
ANDERSON'S SALE

Until the advent of the bulldozer and rubber-tyred dumper all heavy civil engineering work made use in one way or another of railways. The NDCJLR was a small contract, when compared with those of the main-line railways built in the preceding hundred years, but the amount of equipment used was quite surprising. Some was bought new but other was brought in from earlier contracts.

P. & W. Anderson Ltd were put into liquidation by the company's debenture holders during the course of the NDCJLR contract and when work was completed the Receiver, Mr F. Maloney, put all the plant and equipment up for sale. The auction was dealt with by J. T. Skelding & Co, of London, and the 800 plus lots were sold over three days, commencing 9 September 1925. The auction catalogue, with its detailed lists, gives a very good idea of the amount of equipment needed to construct a relatively simple branch line. Most of it was dumped adjacent to the newly constructed Marland siding on NDCC land.

The auction started on the Wednesday morning innocuously enough with 'Lot 1 - Three lengths of rubber hose pipe and 24 cement bags' and continued through a vast range of engineering jumble and ironmongery to conclude with 128 one-yard capacity two-feet gauge side- and end-tipping wagons, plus a few spares. In between were included 114 shovels and 144 picks, a 3-ton steam derrick, a 2-ton hand derrick, a sawbench, lathe, vertical drilling machine and a grinding machine from the workshop, two jawcrushers, two horizontal steam engines, two steam pumps, four blacksmiths forges and two gent's safety bicycles.

On Thursday, after disposing of some tubing, tanks and timber, the main attraction was track. Enough two-feet gauge portable track and rails, of 14lb. 16lb and 20lb sections, and sleepers were for sale to make $2^3/_4$ miles (4.5km) of track. Heavier rail sections, 30lb, 40lb, 50lb and 60lb, were used for the larger gauges and these totalled more than three miles.

Friday was the most interesting day. Standard gauge wagons were listed first; 19 M.S.C. side- and end-tip wagons and a dozen ballast wagons. On the three-feet gauge were 52 M.S.C. wagons and six rail bogies. (The ubiquitous type of contractors wagon took its name from the Manchester Ship Canal contract where more than 6,000 of them were used). The first locomotive was the two-feet gauge *Western Lea*, later bought by the Meeth (North Devon) Clay Co. Ltd, and described in Chapter 10. Three four-coupled locomotives were of three-feet gauge - *Bunty, Gyp,* and *Alston* - while the standard gauge also had three locomotives - a four-coupled named *Birkenhead* and two un-named six-coupleds. Also on the two-feet gauge was an Austro-Daimler petrol locomotive, said to be by Du Cros and Brauns, although these must have been suppliers not manufacturers. The locomotives are summarised at the end of this Appendix.

Three vertical boilers were also for sale. The company's motor transport for the contract consisted of a Ford 5-seater touring car, fitted with a 'cape-cart hood', registration T5990, a Maxwell 5-seater touring car, registration MS2567 and a $2^1/_4$ h.p. New Hudson motor-cycle, registration TA6685.

The surveying equipment included two theodolites, three levels and a dumpy level plus several tapes, chains and ranging rods.

Adjoining Meeth station were the accommodation huts that had caused so much trouble a couple of years before. The smaller was 24 feet 3 inches by 15 feet 6 inches but the larger was 93 feet long by 16 feet 4 inches wide plus three 'annexes' of varying sizes. There was a double-oven cooking range and - indicative of the navvies fare - a 10 gallon cast-iron 'Farm Boiler'. Nearby were a shelter, an earth closet and a latrine, all rough-boarded. At Venton level crossing were the carpenters' shop, smiths' and engineers' shop and a couple of stores.

The office was at 39 Well Street, Torrington, and its furniture included the usual desks, chairs and stools, a safe and a typewriter but also two military washstands. A surprising item in the office was a gelignite warming pan but the inclusion of a 0.320 six-chamber revolver and cartridges was not when one remembers the troubles at Hatherleigh.

How successful the sale was is not known. Both *Western Lea* and No 79 remained at the siding for a further couple of months before being bought and no doubt other equipment remained unsold. Meeth bought some rails at the sale but both works probably had adequate wagons and equipment for their needs and were not able to take advantage of the sale on their doorstep.

(l am indebted to the late B. D. Stoyel for the loan of the Sale Catalogue from which these details are drawn.)

APPENDIX FOUR

Summary of locomotives used on NDCJLR contract:

Gauge	Plant No	Name	Type	Manufacturer	No	Date	Cylinders (Inches)	Driving Wheels	Wheel-base	Notes
2ft	151	*Western Lea*	0-6-0WT	Hudswell Clarke	1314	1918	6½ x 12	1'11½"	4'2"	(a)
2ft			?	Austro-Daimler		?	Petrol			
3ft	36	*Bunty*	0-4-0IST	Bagnall	1480	1897	8 x 12	1'11½"	3'6"	
3ft	51	*Alston*	0-4-0IST	Bagnall	1434	1894	8 x 12	2'	3'6"	
3ft	52	*Gyp*	0-4-0T	Barclay	761	1895	6 x 12	1'9"	3'6"	
Std	79	*(Ardwick)*	0-6-0ST	Manning Wardle	1049	1888	12 x 18	2'11"	10'10"	(b)
Std	186	*Birkenhead*	0-4-0ST	Hudswell Clarke	650	1903	10 x 16	2'9½"	5'7"	
Std	244		0-6-0ST	Manning Wardle	1153	1890	12 x 18	2'11½"	10'10"	

(a) to Meeth (North Devon) Clay Co. Ltd.
(b) to North Devon Clay Co. Ltd.

ACKNOWLEDGEMENTS

One of the pleasures of writing this book and the research it involved was the eager and willing assistance that so many gave me, both in an individual and a corporate capacity. The historian is not the greatest boon to a modern commercial operation but at both Marland and Meeth, and at what were the respective head offices, Newton Abbot and St Austell, when the first edition was written, I was welcomed with courtesy and a real interest. And this pleasure has been repeated, more than twenty years later, for this second edition.

For the first edition I had great help from the late C. D. Pike, OBE, MA, LLB, then Chairman of WBB, his son John Pike and the company secretary D. A. Norman FCA, while at Marland Tom Birchall and George Copp gave enthusiastic interest. Of the English China Clays Group; Graham Rowsell, Assistant Secretary, and Colin Yelland, of the Estates Department, both at John Keay House, E. R. Johnson, Production Director, and John Lloyd and R. B. Jotcham at Meeth were most helpful.

Former employees helped in ways that no archive could. The late E. A. Holwill, former Managing Director of the North Devon Clay Co. Ltd, and Mrs Holwill, were very hospitable on numerous occasions, always ready to answer with great care and consideration my endless questions, and to answer my letters which frequently must have more resembled examination papers. Mr Holwill also read that part of the first manuscript relating to the NDCC. Lou Stacey and Tom Vallance, both retired from Meeth, were kind enough to fill my tape recorder with all sorts of useful information.

At the more usual places of enquiry I must thank the staff at the Devon Record Office; the staffs of the Public Record Office; the British Library; the House of Lords Records Office; University College Library, Cardiff; the North Devon Athenaeum, Barnstaple; Companies House, Cardiff and London; Angela Broome, Librarian of the Royal Institution of Cornwall; D. C. Phillips, University of Reading Institute of Agricultural History and Dr R. P. Lee, Hon. Librarian of the Narrow Gauge Railway Society.

Despite the narrow scope of this book one's ignorance on certain matters, locomotives in particular, soon becomes apparent and I am grateful for a wide circle of friends and acquaintances who have helped in one way or another. They are listed below in alphabetical order and if my memory or filing system have failed me I can only apologise: Rowland Abbott; Allan C. Baker; C. R. Clinker; Barry Hughes; Alistair Jeffrey; Frank Jux; Dr M. J. T. Lewis; W. J. Passmore; K. P. Plant; Douglas Pointon; R. N. Redman; S. J. Rhodes, formerly of Real Photographs Co. Ltd.; B. D. Stoyel; Michael Stratton; E. A. Wade; Russell Wear; C. R. Weaver and W. K. Williams. Two corporate bodies must be added to this list of individuals; London Transport, through their Publicity Officer, and Hunslet (Holdings) Ltd.

This second edition has enabled me to renew old acquaintances, and despite the many changes, corporate and otherwise, a warm and enthusiastic welcome has been given me. One negative point is that 'Health and Safety' now rules the day and no longer can the casual exploration of the moors and workings be enjoyed, as in the 1960s. Another is that, sadly, many of those mentioned above are no longer with us. Others have retired or moved on.

George Copp, now retired works manager from Marland, has an enthusiasm that never dims and cheerfully answers questions or seeks out information. Kevin Bennett, of WBB Minerals at Marland, has taken great pains to bring me up to date with developments there while Ivor Bowditch of Imerys plc has done the same for me regarding Meeth. E. A. Holwill's son, A. P. Holwill and J. H. Holwill's son, W. J. Holwill, have helped with the family background. John Pike is now custodian of the Ball Clay Heritage Society archive and has generously given me access to this as well as assisting with photographic sources. Barry Hughes has provided valuable information from his own collection and from the North Devon Museum Trust collection. A number of people have helped with information and made their own research available and I thank Michael Bishop; Martin Bodman; Colin Brown, Seaton Tramway; Dr Harry Cramp, Torrington & District Historical Society; Matthew Gicquel, Devon Railway Centre; Richard Jotcham, formerly at Meeth; John Nicholas; F. Keith Pearson; R. Pooley; Eric Shepherd.

The photographic sources are detailed in the captions but I must make especial mention of John Allsop; Richard Casserley; Barry Hughes; Roger Kidner; Alan Stoyel; John and Jane Townsend and Lyn Williams (Beaford Centre). The late Ted Wade deserves the major credit for the locomotive and rolling stock drawings, produced especially for this book despite many commitments of his own. Roger West was kind enough to offer to amend his drawing to represent a Marland locomotive.

ACKNOWLEDGEMENTS

The late Harry Paar read the first edition manuscript and his guidance and willing assistance in filling gaps in my own research was much appreciated. Dr Peter Stanier has read the second edition manuscript and made sure that the new blends with the old. As with the first edition, Chris Tilley has been a willing partner with his practical assistance in aiding and abetting my researches. I have a great debt of gratitude to Alan Kittridge who has not only designed this edition but has put a great deal of work into preparing photographs and drawings for publication.

This book has no dedication but if it did it would have had to be to the Holwill family - to Frederick, to Henry and even to Eustace - who started it all and gave me the story, and to E. A. Holwill who saw the old order finish and who has given me so much to write down.

Sources

The sources for this history have been many and varied and no single record can be identified as the major source. I have been fortunate in that several important archives have not been available before, both for the first and second editions. The NDCJLR Minutes only became available, under the 30 year rule, in 1978 and details of the closure of the line have emerged since. A number of valuable files of NDCC correspondence, that had been saved from oblivion, were loaned to me as were some quite important documents in private hands. Unlisted here but no less valuable have been the memories of E. A. Holwill, L. Stacey, and T. Vallance, with between them some 140 years in the clay industry.

A problem in giving locations of sources for this second edition is that many have changed and it has not proved practical to establish the exact present whereabouts of all. As a result of my interest WBB deposited many North Devon Clay Company papers with the North Devon Record Office at Barnstaple, and the Ball Clay Heritage Society also has a number of papers. Imerys plc has handed over many papers relating to Meeth to the China Clay Historical Society, whose archives are at Wheal Martyn, Cornwall. The papers of the Meeth (North Devon) Clay Company that I rescued from the derelict office at Woolladon are now deposited with the North Devon Record Office also.

Because of the diversity of sources, and the fact that some of the most useful were totally uncatalogued, it did not prove practical to give sources directly by footnote, but the majority are listed below, together with an indication of their whereabouts where practicable. Not all are accessible to the public. The following abbreviations are used:

BCHS	Ball Clay Heritage Society, Newton Abbot
BL	British Library
CRO	Companies Registration Office, Cardiff
DRO	Devon Record Office, Exeter
NDRO	North Devon Record Office, Barnstaple
TNA	The National Archives (formerly Public Record Office), Kew

1. Documentary and Archive Sources:

North Devon Clay Co. Ltd.
Company file, 1893 onwards (CR0)
Deeds & Agreements, sundry documents
Report by John Bilton 1892 (BCHS)
Prospectus 1893
Inventory & Valuation 1937
Report by W. J. & C. P. Bates 1948
Minute Books, General Meetings & Directors
Correspondence files

Marland Brick & Clay Works Ltd.
Company file, 1879 - 1888 (TNA)
Bank passbooks, 1880 - 1887

Marland North Devon Brick Co. Ltd.
Company files, 1891 - 1894 (TNA)

Torrington & Marland Railway
Contract drawings, 1879 (DRO)
Sundry Agreements, correspondence & leases (DRO)
Correspondence files

North Devon & Cornwall Junction Light Railway
Deposited Plans, 1909 & 1910 (DRO)
Light Railway Order 1914 (DRO)
Light Railway (Amendment) Order 1922 (DRO)
Light Railway (Extension of time) Order 1923 (DRO)
Minute Books, Directors (TNA)
Ministry of Transport papers (TNA)
British Railways Board papers (TNA)
Inspection Report by Major C. L. Hall, 1925 (TNA)
Agreements & Historical File (TNA)
NDCC Correspondence files (WBB)

Bideford & Tavistock Railway
Deposited Plans, 1845 (DRO)

Okehampton Railway
Deposited Plans, 1864 & 1866 (DRO)
NDCC Correspondence files

Torrington & Okehampton Railway
Deposited Plans, 1895, 1896 & 1898 (DRO)
NDCC Correspondence files
Acts of Parliament, 1895, 1898, 1901 & 1907

John Barraclough Fell
Patent No 1014 of 1873
Patent No 1638 of 1879
Patent No 1249 of 1880

Meeth (North Devon) Clay Co. Ltd.
Company file, 1919 - 1979 (CRO)
Minute Books, Directors
Deeds & Agreements, sundry papers
Correspondence files (NDRO)

2. BOOKS AND PRINTED WORKS:

Brandram-Jones, H.	'A Railway on a Budget' *Tenterden Terrier* Winter 1976
Geological Survey	*Ball Clays* 1929
Grieves, Keith	*Sir Eric Geddes* 1989
Hadfield, E. C. R.	*The Canals of South West England* 1967
Harrods	*Directory of Devon* 1878
Hateley, R. (Ed)	*Industrial Locomotives of South West England* 1977
Hughes, Barry D.	*Rolle Canal & The North Devon Limestone Trade* 2006
Hutchings, W. J.	*Out of the Blue* (1956)
Kelly's	*Directory of Devonshire* various issues
Lysons	*Magna Britannia* 1822
Nicholas, John	*Lines to Torrington* 1984
Polwhele, R.	*The History of Devonshire* 1797
Rolt, L. T. C.	*The Potters Field* 1974
Scrutton, Susan	*Lord Rolle's Canal* 2006
Swete, John	*Travels in Georgian Devon; the illustrated journals of the Reverend John Swete, vol III* 1999

Thomas, D. StJ.	*Regional History of the Railways of Great Britain, Vol.1 The West Country* 1960
Thomas, D. StJ.	*North Devon Railway Report* 1963
Tonks, E. S.	*Ruston & Hornsby Locomotives* 1974
Wade, E. A.	*The Patent Railways of John Barraclough Fell* 1986
Wear, R. & Lees, E.	*Stephen Lewin and the Poole Foundry* 1978
White, W.	*Directory of Devonshire* 1850, 1878

3. NEWSPAPERS AND PERIODICALS

Bideford Weekly Gazette, 1879 - 1923
The Brickbuilder, April 1898 (Supplement to the British Clayworker)
The Devon Historian, 1971
The Devon Weekly Times, 1900
Devonshire Association, Transactions of 1879, 1890, 1891, 1902, 1904, 1955
The Financial Times, 31 August 1900
Geological Society of London, Quarterly Journal of 1864, 1878
'*Hansard*', 1919 - 1923
The Industrial Railway Record, Nos. 36, 42, 81 (1971 - 1979)
The Locomotive, 15 July 1913
Machinery Market, 1 May 1882
The Narrow Gauge, No 76
Narrow Gauge News, 1962, 1966 - 1969, 1971
North Devon Journal, 1893 - 1925
Okehampton Post, 1925
The Pottery Gazette & Glass Trade Review, 1 May 1923
Railway Magazine, 1925
Railway World, 1946, 1952, 1953, 1960
Western Morning News, 1881, 1953
Western Times, 1925

4. MAPS

Tithe map. Petersmarland parish (DRO)
Tithe map. Petrockstow parish (DRO)
Ordnance Survey. 1st Edition 6-inch & 25-inch maps (BL & DRO)
Ordnance Survey. 2nd Edition 6-inch & 25-inch maps (DRO)
Clinton Estate Maps 1958 (BCHS)

INDEX

Accidents   26, 31, 34, 51, 82
Anderson, P. & W. Ltd   33-4, 43, 49, 58, 63, 69 *et seq.*, 77, 93, 99, 100, 110
Annery   8
Ball clay   5, 7, 8, 102
Barley Hayes   43-4, 102
Barnstaple   7, 26, 65, 72, 83, 90
Bideford   5, 7-9, 15, 20, 21, 65-6, 69-72, 75, 79, 98
Black Torrington   8, 28
Brick trade & manufacture   7, 8, 9 *et seq.*, 25 *et seq.*, 66, 81, 101
Bude   65
Bury Moor   6, 8, 13, 15, 28, 29, 34, 35, 65, 71
Capital   10, 11, 13, 17, 18, 20, 66-7, 77, 91-2, 98
Clay Moor   8, 9, 13, 34, 65
Clay pits   11, 14, 16-17, 29, 82, 94-5, 98
Couplings   47, 53, 61, 62
Devon County Council   71-2, 94, 98
Dunsbear   28, 29, 34-6, 44, 60, 71, 79, 80, 86-8, 102
ECC Ball Clays Ltd   98, 102
Electricity   18, 96
Employees   11, 34, 81, 94, 106-7
English China Clays Ltd   96, 98
Export trade   7, 20, 21, 94, 98
Fowey   16, 19, 90, 98
Fremington   7, 15, 16, 36, 64-6, 88
Geology   8
Grange Moor   36, 39
Green Odd Railway & General Contracting Co. Ltd.   25
Halwill Junction   65-6, 71, 73, 75, 77, 78-9, 81, 85-8, 92-3, 102
Hatherleigh   8, 27-8, 65-6, 70-6, 78-9, 81-3, 86, 88, 94, 102
Hexter & Budge Ltd.   98
Hodge Bros./Marcus Hodges & Sons   17, 21, 47, 55, 60, 62
Hole   78-9, 81, 83, 86-7, 102
Holsworthy   66, 71, 92
Imerys   98, 102
Labour, Ministry of   74-7
Langtree Wick   43, 45
Light railways   6, 25-7, 41-2, 66, 69, 72-3, 90
Locomotives:
    contractors   33-4, 43, 58, 69-71, 77, 93, 99-100, 110-11
    main line   82 *et seq.*
    narrow gauge   33, 47 *et seq.*, 109
    standard gauge   36, 57 *et seq.*, 109
Machinery   10, 11, 14, 91 *et seq.*
Marland   5, 7-8, 9 *et seq.*, 28, 66, 71, 91, 95, 99, 102
Marland Brick & Clay Works Ltd.   9-11, 25
Marland North Devon Brick Co. Ltd.   11-14
Meeth   5-6, 7-8, 16, 71, 77-80, 84, 86, 91 *et seq.*, 102
Meeth Ball Clays (ECC) Ltd.   98
Meeth (North Devon) Clay Co. Ltd.   16, 73-4, 77, 79, 89-90, 91 *et seq.*, 99 *et seq.*, 102, 109, 110
Monmouth & South Wales Colliery Owners Pitwood Association   99

INDEX

Nationalisation   86
Newton Abbot Clays Ltd.   91 *et seq.*
North Devon & Cornwall Junction Light Railway   5, 15, 33, 35, 40, 43, 44, 46, 65, 69 *et seq.*, 79 *et seq.*, 91-3, 102, 108
North Devon Clay Co. (Ltd)   8, 11 *et seq.*, 28, 66, 75, 102, 109
North Devon Pottery   8, 10
North Tawton   92
Okehampton   65-6, 71, 73, 81, 92, 99
Operating methods (railway)   29, 34, 106-7
Passenger traffic   5, 31, 35, 60, 65, 80-1, 83, 86, 87-8
Passmore & Sons   92-3
Pencleave Valley   45, 65-6, 80, 88
Permanent way   17, 23, 25, 26, 31, 34, 34-7, 41 *et seq.*, 47, 55, 63, 73, 79, 81, 87, 103-5, 108, 110
Peters Marland   8,9
Petrockstow   7-8, 9, 65-6, 78 *et seq.*, 88, 102
Pipe-clay   7-8, 9, 65
Potteries   7-8, 10, 94, 95
Processes   11, 19, 95
Production   11, 14 *et seq.*, 21, 28, 33, 66, 73, 81, 92, 94, 96, 98, 101, 102
Public traffic   29, 31, 34, 39, 108
Pumping   9, 16, 18, 92, 110
Purbeck   8
Railways (other than T&MR and NDCJLR):
    Bideford and Tavistock   8, 65, 66
    Bodmin & Wenford   59
    Devon & Cornwall Central   65
    Llanberis Lake   38
    London & South Western   8, 9, 26, 29, 65, 66, 71 *et seq.*, 77, 79, 81
    Lynton & Barnstaple   5, 15, 38
    North Cornwall   70
    North Metropolitan Tramways   60
    Okehampton   65
    Pentewan   42
    Plymouth & North Devon Direct see Torrington & Okehampton
    Seaton & District Electric Tramway   38, 57, 60, 63
    Southern   34, 35, 64, 77, 79 *et seq.*, 93
    Torrington & Okehampton   6, 15, 65-7, 108
Road traffic   21, 34, 72-3, 81, 86, 90, 92-3, 98
Rolle Canal/Road   8, 9, 27, 35, 45, 46, 65, 79
Rolling stock:
    narrow gauge   17, 47 *et seq.*, 75, 99 *et seq.*
    standard gauge   31, 36, 64, 83, 90
Sampford Courtenay   27-8, 65-6, 92
SCR - Sibelco   21, 102
Shipping   9, 15-16, 19, 20-1, 88
Sidings: narrow gauge   25, 28-9, 34-5, 36, 37, 105
    standard gauge   36, 59, 73, 78-82, 87-90, 92-4
Signalling   25, 29, 36, 79, 83, 86, 88
South Devon   7-8, 20-1, 66, 91, 98
Speccott   43-5
Steam engines, stationary and portable   11, 12, 15, 37, 47, 55, 92, 110
Stockleigh   71, 91-2, 94, 98
Stowford Moor   27, 34, 43-4, 46, 65
Summit   27-9, 31, 34, 80, 102

Teignmouth   21, 90, 98
Terra cotta   2, 10, 11, 14, 18
Torridge, River   32 *et seq.*, 43 *et seq.*, 65, 69-71, 76, 77, 79-81, 88, 102, 103-7
Torrington   7-8, 16, 18, 25 *et seq.*, 31, 34, 35, 65 *et seq.*, 70 *et seq.*, 79 *et seq.*, 90, 99, 102, 103,110
Torrington & Marland Railway   5, 25 *et seq.*, 42 *et seq.*, 47 *et seq.*, 69, 71, 74, 79, 102, 103 *et seq.*, 108, 109
Traffic figures   34, 39, 81-2, 84, 86, 108
Tram-cars   31-2, 60, 61
Transport, Ministry of   72, 74-5, 77, 88
Trans-shipment   22, 36, 62, 94, 102, 108
H.M. Treasury   71, 73-4
Underground working   15, 19-20, 37, 94-5
Unemployment   71, 73-4, 90
Ventilation   18
Viaducts   25-7, 33-5, 41 *et seq.*, 47, 55, 69-70, 77, 79-80, 102, 103 *et seq.*, 109
War, Great   16, 33, 50, 53, 71-2, 99, 100, 108
War, Second World   18, 19, 98
Watergate   27-9, 34, 37, 43, 65, 78, 79, 81, 87, 102
Waterwheel   16
Watts Blake Bearne & Co. Ltd. (WBB)   20, 21, 98, 102
Wear Gifford   7-8, 9, 65
Wedgwood   7
Western Morning News   74-5
Wolstanton Ltd.   94
Woolladon   65, 71, 91 *et seq.*, 94, 100-1
Workmen's trains   2, 9, 29, 31, 34-6, 60, 67, 108
Yarde   6, 28, 29, 31, 34-5, 43-5, 60, 70, 78, 80-1, 84, 86, 88, 102

PEOPLE:
Babb, Sargeant   76
Balsdon, William   74, 91, 94
Braginton, George   8, 9
Brain, W. H.   95-6
Channon, C. J.   76, 92-6
Clinton, Lord   8, 13, 25, 29, 67, 84
Cobbledick, James   92
Corn, E. R.   95-6
Crediton, Bishop of   76
Donne, T. S.   91, 98
Fell, G. N.   26, 28, 34, 47, 106-7
Fell, J. B.   6, 10, 25 *et seq.*, 41 *et seq.*, 47, 48, 61, 66, 103 *et seq.*
French, R. R.   91 *et seq.*
Geddes, Sir Eric Campbell   72, 90
Greening family   9
Griffiths, Capt. J. H. T.   75, 92
Grover, Major   27
Hall, Major G. L.   77, 79-80
Hancock, E. J.   91, 93, 98
Holbrook, H. H.   73
Holwill, E. A.   18, 19, 31, 36
Holwill, Eustace   13-14, 91-3, 99
Holwill, Frederick   8, 9-11, 25
Holwill, Henry   10-11, 13, 15-16, 18, 29, 31, 33-4, 44, 47, 51, 53, 57, 69, 72, 74-5, 91

INDEX

Hooper, J. T.   91-2
Hopkins, Rice & Thomas   65
Hopkins, Roger   65
Hutchings, W. J.   76
Jervis, James T.   66
Johns, Samuel   27
Lambert, George MP   76
Lawton, William   11, 28-9
Limpus, J. M.   11
Lovering, John   91, 93, 98
Ludlam, J. W.   10-11, 28
Martin, 'Ganger'   17, 18
Maxwell family   8, 10
Moore Stevens, J. C.   25, 71
Neal, Arthur MP   75
Oag, James   70
Peto, Basil MP   75
Phillips, J. J.   94
Rowland, Frederick   82
Sanders, Henry   31
Scott, Dr Alex   94
Sillifant, John   18
Stephens, H. F.   16, 33, 35, 57, 69 *et seq.*, 77, 79, 84, 93, 99
Walker, Sir Herbert   73
Wren family   9
Wren, W. A. B.   9-11, 13, 25, 28
Wren, the Misses E. S. & D. M.   13, 15, 47, 108
Yee, Fung   27

This recently discovered photograph was taken about 1920 at the same time as those on pages 9 and 17, and in fact depicts the same shaft head as page 17. This is presumably the team responsible for this shaft. The method of tipping the skip bucket can be clearly seen. A rough shelter is behind the men, to the left of the shaft.
BALL CLAY HERITAGE SOCIETY